FISHIN
FU

CW00435351

J. Johnston Mann

ARTHUR H. STOCKWELL LTD.
Elms Court   Ilfracombe
Devon

By the same author:
The Art of Dapping

Edited by Mrs Gillian Dennison

Front cover by kind permission of
SCOT RAIL

ISBN 0 7223 2181-3
Printed in Great Britain by
Arthur H. Stockwell Ltd.
Elms Court   Ilfracombe
Devon

FISHING FOR FUN

For some time past many of my friends, and some who have actually been involved in some of the incidents related, have suggested that they should have a wider hearing. Encouraged by their suggestion I decided to put pen to paper, resulting in a book entitled *Fishing for Fun,* which hopefully will be enjoyed by anglers and other readers alike.

*Dedication to
Charlie and Sadie
and in memory of
my parents*

CONTENTS

Fishing For Fun	7
A Fishy *Faux Pas*	13
Ghillies	14
Desert Island Discs	15
Packed Lunches	16
A Day On A Hill Loch	18
Over The Sea To North Uist	20
Fishing On Your Doorstep	22
The Right Boat For A Loch	24
My Open Aviary	27
Sandy	31
Long Odds	34
Do Women Make Good Anglers?	37
Boats And Boatmanship	39
Poaching	43
The Wrong Turning	46
Do They Go Together	48
A Tit For Tat	50
The Art Of Trolling	51
Pike	56
Skippy and Beanie	58
"A Colossal Coincidence"	61
Twenty Years Ago	65
Metal Fatigue And Miracles	66
Freak Waves	69
Care Of Tackle	72
Competitive Angling	74
Questionable Friends	76
Outboard Motors	78
Anglers, Fishermen And Tackle	80
Danger Ahead	83
Loch Shiel Past And Present	85
A Mixed Bag	88

FISHING FOR FUN

It is difficult for me to remember when I first became an angler but a glance through the family album produced a photograph of me in the arms of my nurse, with my elder brother nearby; my mother was on the oars, and father ready to shove the boat off the shore. From this evidence I have concluded that I was that day introduced to the pleasurable art of angling — but I was far from becoming one.

As years passed, the water attracted me more and more, and it was not long before I acquired a rod of sorts, cut from a hazel bush; a short line, and a hook attached to a short length of gut. Worms were easy to come by and there were hill burns in plenty but the river Balvaig was out of bounds for the time being — although many a lovely speckled brown trout taken from the burns landed up on the breakfast table; they were pink fleshed, fried in bacon fat and covered in oatmeal, sweet to taste and a good start to the day.

One epic day produced so many trout that the whole family enjoyed them to the full. It happened that road repairs had necessitated the diversion or damming of the water flow, resulting in a burn that ran by the side of the road becoming dried up, leaving shallow pools in which the trout were splashing around because there was not sufficient depth of water to cover their backs. The wee beauties were there for the taking — not a very sporting way of obtaining a basket, but we were very young at the time.

We went on holiday each year to Munro's Hotel, Strathyre, for twenty-one years in all, so we got to know the locals quite well. One was Mr Lyon, the artist; rather a pompus type, who was wont to saunter down to the bridge each morning, smoking a cigarette in a long holder which did not protrude in front of him as much as his ample paunch, but very nearly. When asked what he thought of the Mann boys he replied, "Charlie is a nice laddie, and Alick is a bright wee spud, but I cannot abide that sarcastic bugger Johnston." Well, well, well, at the age of ten years, quite an indictment.

In those days it was a matter of walking the two miles down to the loch. Each morning after breakfast, the anglers would gather at the front of the hotel and proceed down the road, laden with fishing gear and lunch packs, bottles of lemonade and something stronger for those who preferred it. It was Mr Dobbie who liked the latter, and with jaunty step he made his way to the loch, no doubt full of hope for a fruitful day's fishing and an enjoyable lunch; but not so for him, with an almighty bang a brown-tinted froth filtered through his fishing basket, dripping on to the road behind him. I do not know but I hope he caught some trout to compensate for this loss.

At the age of twelve I became ghillie to my father and many were the happy days we spent together, seldom returning to the hotel without some trout. In these far off days there was a good stock of trout, and in the season the salmon rested in Loch Lubnaig before proceeding up the Balvaig to Loch Voil; thence to the many burns which were their spawning grounds.

One day I was suspended from my duties and replaced by the local ghillie, know universally as "Old Corriegowrie", an immense man both in height and girth; his chest was hidden behind a massive beard — a larger one I had never seen.

We were equipped both for fly-fishing and trolling, and as there was little wind it was agreed that trolling was the order of the day. There were no outboard motors then, so "Corrie" bent on the oars and proceeded to take us to the river mouth, where salmon were known to lie; then we trolled along both banks and it was not long before one of the rods bent and the reel screamed like a banshee. In due course a lovely fresh run salmon lay in the bottom of the boat, to be followed by another.

It was obviously going to be our day, and whilst the wind was providing a fresh fishing breeze it was decided to continue with the trolls, which proved a good decision because when we stopped for lunch there were three beauties in the boat.

With this activity, all sense of time had been lost, so it was not until about four o'clock we went ashore for our lunch, only to be urged by "Corrie" to hurry and get back into the boat, which we did. We made several turns round the head of the loch, on the last of which, and within yards of the landing stage, "bang" went the reel again and the fish was duly landed, making four for the day, one of which was my very first salmon. With tackle dismantled we made our way back to the hotel. It was "nae bother" to "Corrie" to carry the four salmon which, when weighed, totalled 23½ lb. "Corrie" was amply rewarded for his day's work; he went back to his croft with a crisp £5 note in his pocket.

Some big catches, however, did not always reach the weighing scales, as happened to my brother and his friend. Both had been fishing a small loch situated in ideal surroundings; scented birch, conifers and giant oak trees came down to the lochside, behind which was was a glorious backdrop of rugged hills covered with fresh green bracken, heather, rowan trees, with gorse in bloom. Not only the setting was perfect, the fishing conditions were as well, with the sun high in the sky and a steady breeze which seemed to float white fleecy clouds before it, covering the sun from time to time; no angler could wish for more.

As the day progressed there was seldom a drift when one or more fish was not caught. As it was hot in the boat they were popped into a bass which was hung from the rowlock over the side; when the drift was finished it was lifted into the boat and then lowered again at the start of the new one. This pattern continued throughout the day until it was time to return to the landing stage. The outboard motor was started up and they proceeded at speed, having forgotten to take the bass inboard; coming alongside and tying up, the tackle was taken up to the car and it only remained to get the bass which was hanging on the far side of the boat. Stretching over the boat the bass was grabbed and lifted up, but there were no fish in it! With the wash of the water the bass had been bumped against the side of boat and it burst, emptying all the trout back into the loch. There are two lessons to be learned from this happening. Firstly, never hang the bass over the side of the boat; secondly, put the fish in a polythene bag and place it out of the sun, or better still under a dampened cloth in the shade beneath the thwart.

Having caught your fish, the cooking should not present a problem. Trout and sea trout, of suitable size, should be placed on their bellies and using a very sharp knife slit down the back, having nicked down each side of the head and tail — now fold down the flesh and skin, and with the knife, remove the flesh from the bone; then grab the tail and with an upward forward movement the bone and the guts will come away easily. Wash and lay the fish flat, salt and pepper the flesh, finally covering it with oatmeal. Pop it into the frying-pan, having heated either fat or oil in it — the result a gentleman's breakfast, winning by a nose from grilled kidney and bacon; kedgeree coming a worthy third.

Having removed the head and tail of a salmon slit the belly from the vent forwards, remove the guts and wash — then cut a section of the shoulder; next cut some steaks, leaving the tail piece. Wrap the shoulder section in foil and put it in salted cold water in the pot; bring to the boil, remove the pot from the stove and leave the fish in the water for ten to fifteen minutes. Unwrap the parcel, and there you have perfectly cooked salmon to be eaten hot or cold. A fresh green salad tossed with a French dressing vinaigrette goes extremely well with salmon.

The steaks should be salted and peppered, and a knob of butter placed on the fish; grill for about seven minutes and turn, grilling the other side for only five minutes. If the fish is properly grilled the flesh near the bone should be a blae colour against the pink of the rest of the steak.

The tail piece should be wrapped in foil after being salted, peppered, and a little butter spread over it, placed in a suitable dish and put into a heated oven about 400°C. Remove after fifteen to twenty minutes, when it should be done to perfection. Serve either hot or cold.

In due course we felt like spreading our wings, and having hired bicycles, we set off to fish the burn which flows into the Balvaig at Balquhidder (the resting place of the famous or infamous, the choice is yours, Rob Roy McGregor). We started fishing a deep dark pool overhung by trees. The water cascaded down rocks ten feet above the pool. We had high hopes for a salmon as it was a well-known resting place for fish; however, it turned out not to be our day, so we left to try further up the burn. There was not much water because of the dry weather; however, we started fishing. At last we came to a slow-running pool, and half-way up it, under a rock ledge, we spotted a big salmon moving its tail just to keep its stance against the flow. The question was how to catch it, we put a juicy worm in front of its nose, but the fish edged away. The tickling of trout in the wee burn around the vicinity had yielded more than a few speckled beauties in the past, so we had a consultation and tossed for who was to try and tickle the big fish. It loved being stroked down its back and around the gills but it was getting us nowhere. With a stick we pushed it out from under the ledge, but the fish resented such rough handling and took off like a rocket into shallow water, scarcely covering its back. We chased it hither and thither up and down the shallow water until it turned downstream with spray everywhere, which in the sun shone like a rainbow. That day we discovered what you are likely to find at the end of it — nothing, well not entirely — it was the end of a splendid day of fun.

Some of the local worthies whom we got to know should not be allowed to escape attention. The local cobbler was "Tackety" McGregor who lived in a tiny cottage two miles outside the village. We used to walk up the road to visit him and were always given glasses of creamy milk straight from the "coo", which was much appreciated.

Still futher along the road was the Kingshouse Inn, the proprietor of which was known throughout the country as having an extensive vocabulary of swear-words, illustrated by the following instances.

My mother called at the inn to enquire about a house that was to let for the summer months; she wanted to get an outside opinion of the property, so she asked the proprietor what he thought about the house. He replied "No M'am the house is not for you, it has boogerish wee windaes the size of your heed."

When the innkeeper's brother was very ill upstairs, the minister was spotted riding his bicycle past the inn. He was suddenly arrested by a shout "Hey Meenister, please come een, there is a booger dying up here and he wants to mack his weel."

It is no wonder that he was known locally as "Booger John".

Glasgow may be miles better now, but it has always been renowned for the numerous salmon, sea trout and brown trout lochs so easily reached by car in one to one and a half-hour's journey both north and south of the city. With eighteen or so to choose from, the citizens in and around Glasgow are a bunch of fortunate anglers. There is no doubt that they utilized those facilities to the full and to good purpose. Loch Vennachar produces some of the finest brown trout, only equal to those of Loch Cluanie, the fighting quality of which can only be compared with those of Loch Leven, which are renowned throughout the world.

(What do you think about it??!)

I think the Lake of Menteith, one of two lakes in Scotland, the other being Presmannan Lake in Berwickshire, no matter whether loch or lake, they are very fishable waters. The latter is unique in that it is tree girt, the branches overhang the water under which trout patrol their own beat, much in the same way as the ladies of Piccadilly do. The boat has to be rowed gently parallel to the shore and choosing a space between the overhanging branches, the fly is dropped in front of the slowly swimming fish, which can be seen opening its mouth and sucking in the fly which you have cast in front of him. With a slight acceleration he moves forward, opens his mouth and from that moment it is up to you whether you net him or not. The odds are much in his favour — the line may get caught up in the branches or he may dart out under the boat to deeper waters. No matter, you have seen a nice trout actually take the fly which must be of extreme interest to the person holding the rod.

Most of the lochs mentioned have well-maintained boats and easy access to landing stages, which is beneficial for those with outboard motors to carry and fix to the boat. For perfection, a fishing hut would be most welcome, but such a thing is pie in the sky; no sooner would it take shape then it would be inhabited by hippies or vandalised by those who have no respect for property. It means that those who want to enjoy comfort in the uncertain weather conditions in Scotland have to do without. Just because a party of so-called anglers who were fishing Loch Cluanie were asked to leave the bar at closing time, they deliberately smashed up the boats. With the planking they lit a fire around which they sat drinking their carry-outs. The damage was discovered in the morning but they had gone so it was useless to call the police. Unfortunately they will return weekend after weekend; they just cannot be stopped. An effort was made by the laird and his two gamekeepers; who told them to get off his property but they ganged up and threatened to throw them into the loch. Fortunately a police car was passing at the time and the crowd was spotted. The officers left the car, went down to the side of the loch, and it was their presence which prevented what might have developed into a nasty incident.

A FISHY *FAUX PAS*

For some time before World War II, I was employed by a well-known tractor manufacturing company and functioned in the territory from Essex to South Wales. In order to save travelling time I purchased a cabin cruiser which was moored at the Trout Inn at Godstow near Oxford. It was there I met the Thames Conservancy Representative, Barclay Morris by name, and it was he who told me about the following incident.

A very exclusive club had the right to fish one of the best-known chalk streams in the district, and, in turn for surreptitiously supervising the fisheries, the local conservancy representative was granted a permit to fish a day or two each year on this supreme water. As the day approached, Barclay traversed the bank in an effort to spot a few worthwhile trout, one of which was in the 3 lb. class.

He was down early on his appointed day and crawled stealthily up the bank and spotted his quarry rising every now and again to the flies floating down on the stream. With great care he cast his fly a foot or two ahead of the great fish, which continued to rise to the natural fly, but ignored the artificial one; after resting a while he tried again but with the same result. While resting again, he smelt tobacco smoke, none other than Balkan Sobrani. He carefully retreated, and, looking over his shoulder, he spied an angler sitting on a shooting-stick; rod spiked into the ground. He was fitted out with fore and aft hat covered in flies; knee and elbow pads; in other words the essence of the immaculate angler.

After exchanging greetings the angler enquired if Barclay had seen any fish activity up on the beat. He mentioned the large trout he had endeavoured to catch and added "I think you should have a 'go' at the old bugger." The angler rose from his shooting-stick and drawing himself to his full height said "Any fisherman who refers to our fish in such language, I will see to it that he never fishes here again, I will report you to the Thames Conservancy Representative," to which Barclay replied "I will be pleased to deal with your complaint personally."

13

GHILLIES

In the main, ghillies are a breed apart. The majority are polite, most helpful, and often have a fund of amusing stories and apt remarks. After a fruitless morning's fishing, one expounded "Sir, everything in our favour is against us."

Occasionally, one meets up with a man who by rights should not have taken the job as a ghillie; totally disinterested in his job, the surroundings, and finally the angler himself. It is up to the ghillie to carry out the instructions given to him; to move the boat out, or in, towards the shore as required, and sometimes row the boat slowly parellel to the shore, so that the angler can cast in towards it, and allow the flies to come round behind the stern. It is a most satisfactory method of fishing, but generally practised with only one in the boat because the bow rod would not have a chance to cast; his line and flies would come round and foul the oars. It is usually when there is a calm, or just a slight breeze, that such a method is used.

When fishing Loch Maree my partner preferred to lie back and enjoy the sun. He told the ghillie to row slowly and allow me to cast towards a steep rock face where the water was very deep; the result was a 3½ lb. brown trout, and two 1½ lb. sea trout. When we returned to the hotel we learnt that no other fish had been caught that day.

Some anglers can be very awkward, but they are immediately spotted by the ghillie. One in this category made such demands on the ghillie it became embarrassing to the other junior member in the boat. Nothing the poor man could do would satisfy the angler, and as the time passed the situation worsened; the only relief came when it was agreed to land for lunch. The boat was rowed shorewards, being guided by the angler who was standing up in the stern in order to get a better view. "Row with your right. Now backwater with your left, steady now, right row" and the ghillie did just that. He pulled hard on both oars, unbalancing the angler who fell backwards into the shallow water. The resulting language prevents me from telling the reader what happened next.

DESERT ISLAND DISCS

In early spring some years ago, the proprietor of the Loch Shiel Hotel could be seen down at the pier painting, varnishing and fitting out his sailing dinghy, which was his pride and joy.

Sometime later I was out fishing in favourable conditions with a steady breeze from the south-west. I happened to look up and saw the dinghy speeding along, then suddenly it stopped having run slap bang onto a sandbank, the sails flapping in the wind. The intrepid yachtsman clambered out with some difficulty over the highly polished foredeck, and just as a gust of wind hit the sails the boat took off, because it was impossible to get a grip on the smooth varnished surface of the deck and restrain it from doing so.

I decided that such a happening was too good to be true, so I returned to the cottage, sat down and wrote a letter supposedly coming from the BBC with an invitation to appear on The Desert Island Discs programme and requesting the titles of the records of his choice, which I handed into the hotel — leaving it with the receptionist saying it was most urgent.

A few days passed then we saw each other at some distance in the village and I received a sideways glance. I determined to visit the hotel that evening and ask the proprietor to join me in a glass of a very drinkable German brandy in the hope of establishing the friendly relationship which had previously existed between us.

They were firmly established, but only after the level of the liquor in the bottle had dropped significantly.

PACKED LUNCHES

Some packed lunches are better than others and even the better ones can be improved with the spice of imagination. Sandwiches do not take any longer to make when adding a choice of a little of this or a little of that.

Basically they are made with white or brown bread and rolls or baps with the necessary fillings, of which there is a large choice.

The method is simple, spread butter on one slice of the bread and a little mayonnaise on the other, place a piece of boiled ham on the bread and several thinly cut slices of apple on the other and then close the two slices together. If you are in a hurry, some Cheddar cheese, with a bite, placed on a buttered slice of brown bread with some chutney on the other slice makes a good sandwich.

Some sardines whipped up in a bowl to which some mayonnaise has been added along with some chopped up hard boiled eggs is an appetizing centre-piece.

If you have not had eggs for breakfast, a buttered bap or roll makes a good case for crisp bacon and an egg fried both sides so that the yolk will not run all over the place.

A raid on the fridge may disclose a nice piece of left-over, slightly underdone roast beef upon which, spread a little mustard. If you have found some cold lamb a touch of red currant jelly is to be recommended before being enclosed between the buttered bread. Pepper and salt should be used to taste.

A buttered bap or roll makes a good casing for scrambled eggs or cold mince spiced with a little gentleman's relish or horseradish sauce. If a dressed crab is available all to the good; a whipped up kipper or any other smoked fish as a filling could satisfy a hungry soul.

For those who prefer it whisky or gin must not be forgotten and a bottle of any of the fizzy drinks for the teetotaller; and lastly plastic mugs are better than glass tumblers because the latter are apt to get broken.

Some people like a "brew-up" either over a quickly made wood fire (not to be kindled anywhere near a forestry plantation), or a 'Volcano' which is a cylindrical tapered tube about 18″ high with a ring on top; the fuel is newspaper shoved up inside the tube; when set alight it will boil the kettle in no time at all. When leaving the site damp down the fire or lay stones on top of it to put it out.

If perchance you have been lucky enough to catch a salmon and there is a smoke house nearby, then the sandwich will move up into the luxury class. Two slices of brown buttered bread are required; lay the thinly cut smoked salmon on to them, then pepper the fish and squirt some lemon juice on it, clap the slices together, and enjoy the king of sandwiches.

All sorts of paté, now becoming readily available in out of the way places, can be enjoyed if spread on either white or brown bread.

In the warmer weather lettuce, tomatoes, spring onions and cucumbers can be used by themselves or to garnish all types of fillings.

A mashed up banana and a little sugar is an unusual sandwich but it really is very nice to eat.

If in your hurry to jump into the car and be off, do not leave your lunch pack on the kitchen table.

B

A DAY ON A HILL LOCH

In the Moidart area near Acharacle there are some very good lime-stone hill lochs and it was one of those our party, consisting of my two brothers and three others, decided to fish on a day of potential promise. We left the hotel, and, in two cars travelled the few miles to the base of the path which climbs very steeply to our chosen loch.

The pathway in the old days was kept in good condition which allowed for taking up fry, freshwater shrimp and special weeds in pannier tanks slung on the backs of ponies. Unfortunately time has eroded the path making it most difficult to walk on, so at times the direct route was through bracken and heather, knee-high in places.

At last the loch came in sight and it was with relief we unloaded our packs, but unnoticed, one member was missing and it was a few minutes before a head appeared over the rise of the ground and then with a sigh he removed his load. In doing so there was a clink of bottles which turned out to be four large screw-top bottles of beer — young brothers make good pack horses.

We tackled up and made our various ways around the lochan looking for spits of land from where to fish. The results were good as we found out when we gathered for lunch and a glass of beer. It was only then did we appreciate the magnificent view in all directions; to the west the Atlantic ocean studded with many islands; to north, east and south, the great hills covered in purple heather against a background of various shades of green and brown. From the small lochans below there were flashes of the rippled reflection of the sun sparkling like yellow diamonds; from others the bluest of blue was reflected from the sky; a carpet of variegated colour. If nothing else such a view was worth the stiff climb.

It was over this succession of small tarns that a golden eagle was spotted flying towards the east. As he passed over the first tarn, a scramble of terns took off in pursuit, but as soon as they reached the end of their patrol, they returned to their nesting site. No sooner had they landed than another flight took to the air and literally dive-bombed the great bird. This was repeated until the eagle, despite his size, and flying at considerable speed, disappeared into one of the few fleecy clouds.

Two of us were fishing from the boat and one raised and caught a fish which stood on its tail and splashed its way to the bank and disappeared into the heather, but it flipped its way back to the water and was duly netted — it weighed 2½ lb.; dark of back, and yellow of belly with red spots on either side as big as the old "ticky" coin long since withdrawn.

Only too soon had we to return; the descent was almost as bad as the upward climb; each step taken jarring the knee joints so that one member of the party decided to glissade down the steeper parts. Without more ado, he folded his waterproof poncho, placed it between his legs and away he went. It is a wonder he did not set the heather on fire, at the speed he was going. He was first down but he had to take his breakfast off the mantelpiece the following morning.

In all it was a most successful day, ending in sitting down to an appetizing meal consisting of sauté of lamb, cauliflower and the most delicious potatoes. They were piled high in the dish, great fluffy balls with a knob of farm butter spread over them. Who could ask for more? The owner of the place had grown these potatoes for years and gained a country-wide reputation for them, but he had unfortunately forgotten the name; even so it is doubtful if they would have grown to perfection anywhere else. There is no doubt the soil at that particular plot had a great deal to do with the quality.

The following day it was decided to fish the loch, so we got into the boats and rested our weary limbs throughout the day.

OVER THE SEA TO NORTH UIST

I have always had the desire to fish the many famous lochs of the Outer Isles. In this I was assisted by my good friend Gordon MacDonald who happened to be a native of Lochmaddy. So we decided to book our flight, and rooms in the Lochmaddy Hotel.

We left Glasgow and were told by the hostess that the flight would be via Stornoway over which town we circled in thick cloud. At last we got clear vision and landed safely. In a few minutes we were on our way to Benbecula which is about ten miles distant from Lochmaddy.

Before the causeway was built, the journey was undertaken in a farm cart when the tide was out, and thereafter in an old banger of a taxi to Lochmaddy. We were told that the cart would not be available for about an hour so we were guided to a cottage where we enjoyed tea and fresh baked scones.

Fortunately the weather was fine and after climbing into the cart we started off for the other side — it was not a comfortable journey but it was eased by listening to the others discussing the local goings on.

The inevitable dram was offered and accepted more than once by the driver, who, when nearing the other side, told us of an American who had crossed a few days earlier. At the end of the journey he produced his wallet and said "Here's a dollar for the horse, a dollar for each wheel and one for you my good man." Whether this was told with a view to getting a handsome tip from us will never be known.

On arrival we booked in, and were shown to our rooms which were adjoining, and so were the waste pipes of the handbasins enabling us to converse with ease. Later we were introduced to our ghillie, Charlie by name, and he proved to be a real character with a fund of stories.

A drink in the bar along with the other guests gave us the

opportunity of listening to the conversation and getting some idea of the catches which had been taken that day. More importantly we had time to assess our fellow companions, at which time the "guessing game" commenced.

Conversations can be easily overheard above the noise of a busy dining-room, and it eventually came to our ears that the red haired one was a business man of some kind, and that the taller fellow was perhaps an army officer; both descriptions wrong. It now came our turn to guess the likely occupations of our fellow guests; we decided on two being civil servants, another something to do with the war office. A little eavesdropping established what the remainder of the party did for their living.

After dinner of soup, and the delighful island mutton, followed by a sweet, I found myself with little to do, so I viewed the visitors' book. In it I spotted a name I knew and the Kidderminster address. Many years ago on a visit to friends I was asked to make up the numbers for the minor counties' cricket team, I agreed and found myself in the position of long-stop behind a very inefficient wicket-keeper.

One of the opposing batsman was a mighty hitter and hit the ball out of the field. A fellow sitting on the fence indicated that the ball was being carried away in a goods' waggon; the railway ran through a cutting alongside the field.

In the bar in the evening I went up to the man who had been the big hitter at the cricket match and said "It is most interesting to meet the batsman who hit the ball out of the field during the minor counties match at Kidderminster some twenty-five years ago." He just looked at me and I could see his mind working, then the penny dropped, and he remarked upon the unusual coincidence. Thereafter we spent a pleasant evening together, chatting mainly about fishing and a little cricket.

All good things come to an end but not before enjoying the morning's fishing on the best of the lochs. As our plane did not leave until late in the afternoon, it was during the flight that Gordon told me that the previous evening he had been pestered by two of the guests to get him to allow them to fish the afternoon session, but they were unlucky; Gordon had told an old friend living locally, that he could have the boat for the afternoon and jolly good luck to him.

FISHING ON YOUR DOORSTEP

The West of Scotland Anglers are a fortunate bunch of lads with good fishing just about an hour's car journey from door to boat. The best of the near lochs are Ard, Vennachar, and Katrine, not to mention the lake of Menteith, which is well stocked with rainbow trout, and it can yield some large indigenous brown trout in the 3 lb. 8 lb. range.

The Pheonix Angling Club used to hold the season's first outing on Loch Ard, which is one of the earliest lochs around Aberfoyle. I had arranged to pick up one of the members, Hugh Clark by name, and take him to the loch as he had no car of his own. It was a warm spring day so the prospects were reasonable. As the day progressed the use of the signals between boats indicated some good catches had been made.

Finally it was agreed to land for lunch on a small island upon which there is a very old building, possibly associated with the monks from the abbey on another island on the lake of Monteith. There is nothing like a morning's fishing to promote a healthy appetite, not to mention a thirst — I produced a flask which my daughter had brought back on her return from Canada; it was plastic and had a screw-top cap and another to seal the liquid. I was busy unpacking my lunch so I said "Hugh help yourself to a dram" and passed the flask to him. As he was about to grasp it, I let it fall and it bounced off the stone floor and then lay at the feet of the hapless Mr Clark who must have thought it was going to be a dramless lunch for him.

On another visit to the loch with my brother, we had a boat on the lower loch, which we proposed to fish, before meeting another rod who was travelling from Edinburgh.

The road drift was considered to be the best. Half-way down there is a large rock protuding from the bank, and it had been reported that a big fish had been sighted nearby. We caught a couple of takeable trout and returned to start the second drift. As we approached, there was a movement in the water and I cast over it. Just as the fly touched the water, a great black head appeared and then sank beneath the surface. I struck and felt the weight of the fish.

It was a long fight which finished up by half-netting and beaching the salmon on the sloping grass bank at the bottom end of the loch. For some days before our trip to the loch there had been very heavy rain which had raised the water level much above average. In consequence the small river between the loch and the river Forth was running as high as possibly it had ever done. This meant the flow over the falls, some distance from the loch, was sufficient to allow salmon to jump them and gain the loch.

As it turned out, that fish was to be the first salmon to be caught in Loch Ard up to that time. In normal weather conditions there is not such a flow of water to permit fish going any further than the pool below the falls, which is shallow with a smooth rock bottom, so preventing a running fish sufficient impetus to get over the top and into the loch above.

My brother had just started up a tackle shop in Glasgow, so we rushed down to Aberfoyle and luckily found a photographer who took a picture of the two of us proudly holding, as far as can be ascertained, the record fish. We reported to ICI the details of the incident because it was the early days of nylon which was slowly replacing the use of gut. The company was extremely interested, and they produced a show-card with the photo and details of the strength of the nylon used and the story of how the salmon was caught. There was hardly a fishing hotel in Scotland that did not have the card on show, much to the benefit of my brother's newly-established enterprise.

THE RIGHT BOAT FOR A LOCH
Reprinted by kind permission of The Gazette Group

'TO make the choice of a boat for loch fishing is no easy task, despite the great number and variety on offer of both wooden and fibre glass construction.

The advantages of wooden boats over those more recently constructed of fibre glass, have to a great extent disappeared, largely due to more advanced designs, simulated clinker built hulls and deeper keels. The rate of drift of the fibre glass boats now compares favourably with that of wooden hulls. In consequence a would-be purchaser can with confidence consider a boat of fibre glass construction.

The author has two, one is a "WITH", 15' 6" × 5' 6" now 12 years old, the other is a "BRISTOL", 15' × 5' 3" which has seen ten seasons. Both were surveyed this year for insurance purposes and they were pronounced as being in excellent condition.

If the weather conditions are favourable in the early part of the year, it is possible to rub down the wood fittings and apply three coats of varnish in three or four days in order to have both boats ready for the opening of the fishing season, which is something which cannot be said in the case of wooden hulls. Further there is no need to allow time for swelling the timbers and possible caulking; even then wooden hulls are apt to leak.

Having made the choice of a boat either made of wood or glass fibre, the purchase of oars, rowlocks and bailer is not enough; there are other purchases to be made to fit it out properly.

A great deal of thought was given to the necessary accessories for both the "WITH" and "BRISTOL" boats and the outcome was as follows.

If only two positions for rowlocks existed then a third was added, complete with rowlocks, so that the boat could be controlled from the bow or stern whilst on the drift, or from the centre position if a big fish is hooked and has to be followed, as is often the case when fishing for salmon and sea trout.

Fitting Out

It is more comfortable to sit on a cross seat, preferably fitted with a "Bumjoy" cushion. The angler is then in a better position for casting or dapping and also for playing a fish, the more so in really rough weather.

Both the cushion and the cross seat should be secured to prevent slipping, the former by elastic straps and the latter by studs screwed to the gunwale, which in turn locate with holes bored in the seat, the ends of which should be shaped to coincide with the curvature of the hull; with no overhang it makes it easier to come alongside the jetty. If the cross seat is not properly secured it can slip off the gunwale, giving the angler a nasty jolt and possibly causing damage to the rods beneath.

The stowing away of waterproof clothing, fishing bags, lunch packs, priest, tools, etc., is always a problem and more so if the rain is coming down in buckets, by which time the waterproof clothing will be put on, but what of the rest of the gear?

This problem was solved by fitting panniers of simple design. Two wooden ends were cut and shaped to conform to the curve of the hull on one side, and the other one was cut straight. Holes were then bored and two aluminium tubes were fitted, cut to a length so that the ends could rest on two of the thwarts. The tubes were spaced a foot apart; around them a waterproof fabric was sewn, leaving a bag in the centre and enough length to make it possble for the ends to be nailed with roofing felt nails to the wooden ends.

Enough length of fabric was again left on the hull side to form a flap to cover the centre bag and an iron bar was sewn into the end of the overlap to secure it in stormy weather.

A rod rest was placed at the stern of the boat enabling surplus rods to be housed with the reels under cover of the flap; the butts resting on the thwart with the tips in the rest.

With a port and starboard pannier fitted, the gear can be stowed thus lessening the risk of damage and increasing the certainty of it being kept dry in all weathers.

A retired admiral remarked when he came ashore that he had never fished from a boat so well and thoughtfully fitted out, adding to his considerable comfort.

The painter should be at least one and a half times the length of the boat as it is sometimes difficult to find a convenient mooring; the additional length may help to solve the problem. It is advisable also to have a piece of wood or iron rod about 3' long, to enable the painter to be secured should the shore line consist of boggy ground: simply shove or hammer the rod into the ground with a stone at an angle and hitch the painter to it. Boats not properly secured have been known to drift away by themselves.

It is an unpleasant feeling to be left high and dry on the shore, watching the boat drift further and further away. It is however, not so bad if there are other boats on the loch at the time, as, in accordance with the unwritten code of practice, the escapee will be taken in tow and returned to the stranded anglers. No doubt a dram would be offered in return for the service rendered.

August, 1981'

The Cottage

The Caravan

The Windvane

The Driveway

MY OPEN AVIARY

When Creel Cottage at Acharacle was built there was not a tree in the ground except the beautiful rows of rowans which grew on either side of the drive down to the shore of Loch Shiel, but there was beneath the rich soil a hard pan of sand, which made a good foundation upon which to construct the cottage — it was not known at the time that the topsoil would promote the prolific growth of the many and varied trees and shrubs which were eventually planted round the outskirts of the site of 1.5 acres and the plot, of some 45 square yards, which was to become the garden.

After settling into the cottage, the creation of the garden was begun entailing the removal of clumps of rush and grass roots, the resultant holes being filled in with squares of turf well trodden down. It was not long before the surface began to look like a lawn as a result of many cuttings and rollings with the mower, then worm-casts began to appear.

It was necessary to plant quick growing trees and shrubs. Leylandii was chosen for the surrounding hedge, whilst scented poplars, willows and pines were planted to surround the larger area of the site. It was never envisaged that they would grow so quickly and give shelter to the garden, and not only to the garden but to the many birds which were now frequenting the area. They were attracted to the short grass and level surface of the lawn which in fact was the only lawn in the whole neighbourhood, where they could obtain worms and grubs. Their diet was well supplemented with household scraps when necessary.

A rarer bird visitor was a sparrow hawk which struck down a blackbird, both disappearing into the hedge, where the unfortunate captive was devoured. Regular visitors were hen harriers, snipe, spotted woodpeckers, blackcap, greenfinch, flycatchers, bullfinch and redpoll, not to mention the twenty-five other varieties. Some came in great flocks in the autumn, especially the red wings, to feast on the rowan, honeysuckle and other berries of which there was plenty to feed on for days.

My fantail pigeons spent their time flying between the cottage and the hotel with a half-way stop at a cottage; the owner having a care for birds, put out food for them so they were well fed. One more greedy than the rest found itself with a necklace of crust around its neck having eaten out the centre of the slice and tipped the crust over its head. I do not suppose it would remain there very long, and a good shower of rain would soften it and it would fall off, so no harm would come to the bird.

In the late autumn great numbers of swans pass overhead, but some settle on the loch to winter in the area. Gaggles of geese, some containing upwards of 120 birds head south to the estuaries of the Forth and Solway where ample food is to be found on the saltings.

The fields surrounding lochs Leven and Daviot are black with the birds much to the consternation of the local farmers.

With such facilities near at hand, it is curious that so few decided to build their nests in the surrounding hedge. In fact, during the time it was possible for the birds to build, about eight years, only two nests were found, there were one or two others which could not be located because of the thickness of the hedge, but the twittering of the young birds proved that they were in existence.

The photograph shows the state of the lawn brought about by one of the most severe draughts experienced in the late 1970s, it was bone hard, so the distribution of grain, bird seed and bread scraps kept some of the birds in the garden for the time being and the others came back after the rains had softened the ground.

It is only fair to mention the other birds which flew over the cottage and its garden; raven, hoodie and black crows, jackdaws, hawks, curlews, gulls, buzzards and finally golden eagles. One of the curlews was struck down by a hawk in a field not thirty yards away from the cottage — I happened to be at the window at the time and saw the burst of feathers and the landing of the two birds, I reached for my camera but was spotted before I could get a picture.

The best sightings of the golden eagles were from the boat when going up the loch; there were only a few cottages on the shore line of the upper reaches, one of which belongs to the well-known writer Mike Tomkies and there were known eyries high up in the crags of the surrounding hills. It was when the young were beginning to fly, together with the parent birds in attendance, that the best viewing was obtained. When fishing a nearby loch I saw eight golden eagles in the air at one time, four parents and four eaglets. It appeared that formal introductions of the youngsters to their near neighbours were

The Swan

The Pigeon

Bird of Prey

Beanie

being made. The existence of the birds in the area was confirmed by the gamekeeper of the estate, with whom I became quite friendly. My report of the sighting to *The Field* was duly published.

It would seem strange with so many birds around the cottage, if, at sometime, a casualty was not brought in for treatment. In time I was handed a very young blackbird in its nest, which had been found floating in a back water of the local burn; a Moses in the bulrushes effect; by a village lad who could not look after it himself as he had to attend school.

With a set of tweezers, a supply of bread soaked in milk and some mince — feeding sessions began. It showed no fear, and soon realised who his foster-parent was; every time it heard my footsteps, the chirping commenced and only stopped when with full belly it fell asleep in its nest.

Its growth was rapid, with fluffy down being replaced by dark feathers in no time at all. Then came the day when it stood on the edge of the nest and flapped its wings. I approached the cottage and whistled but there was no response. I immediately thought about cats, of which there were a number in the vicinity. It was not long before the wee thing appeared from under the caravan and the chirping for food commenced.

By this time the news had got around on the grapevine, and not only my tenants, but other local people came to see it being fed, or just sitting on the lower half of the Belfast door of the caravan. There must be many photographs of the birds in albums through the country.

If I was on the loch or away for any length of time the bird would enter the caravan by way of the ventilator in search of any crumbs in the galley; it did not fly off when I entered but just stood waiting to be fed and then he would go about his own business.

Should the door be shut, it would pop in through the skylight, sometimes to the consternation of my wee dog Sandy, who resented the intrusion into what he claimed to be his rightful domain; with a flurry of wings the dark shadow would then disappear from whence it came.

Finally the time came for me to pack up and return to Glasgow with the troubled thought in my mind, as to who would feed the bird in my absence. I comforted myself with the knowledge that it had not been coming round as often as previously and was feeding on a more natural diet. Sadly, on my return to the cottage in the spring there was no sign of it.

I reported to *The Field* having seen a greenfinch flying with a number of chaffinch weeks after the migration of the main flock which had been around all summer. In the first week of April, I spotted the bird still in the company of the chaffinches and this happened for the next five years. Generally it was not until the middle or end of May that they returned in their numbers, so it can be taken the bird had spent the winter with the chaffinches over the five-year period.

It is not often one can sit in a caravan and witness a bird of prey strike down a chaffinch only a matter of feet from the window, but as the photo shows the culprit, a hen harrier sitting on the fence digesting its prey.

It happened in a flash, a flurry of feathers and the wee bird was borne to the ground; in a few minutes only a few feathers were left to show what had happened.

A day or two later exactly the same thing happened, but on this occasion the prey disappeared into the bushes just in time and a disappointed hunter flew away.

Some time later a fellow angler, who is a keen ornithologist reported witnessing a sad event. He had been keeping an eye on the black-throated diver parent birds and the two chicks; one of them had swam some distance from the others, when out of the sky dived a greater black gull, of which there are many around the loch, and snatched the wee bird from the water. It disappeared down the loch no doubt to its nest (with the chick) to feed the young gulls.

SANDY

It will be about sixteen years since I last fished Loch Monar and it was there I found Sandy. He was half Jack Russell and Border Terrier, a lethal mixture if ever there was one, but it was only on occasions that it showed up. When people approached him, they did not always let the dog have time to show whether or not the person in question was accepted by him.

It was during that trip that Sandy was first introduced to the boat and fishing. It was evident from the start that the sport was for him. Almost at once he stationed himself between my knees on the cross seat and concentrated on watching the dapped fly crossing from side to side. When he saw a fish rising he growled deep down in his throat and got very excited when it was being played, and more so when it was brought into the boat.

He was really very good with the fishers I took out in the boat, but he did have a finger or two; it was a warning bite, just enough to indicate "This far and no further".

It was not long before he thought he was the skipper of the boat and that I was his No. 1. It was decided to take him down a peg. He had got into the habit of sitting up on the small triangular piece right at the bow of the boat and I was frightened that he might fall overboard and get hurt by the propellor, so he had his lesson coming to him in no mean way.

At One Tree Bay there was a sandbank where the depth of the water, shore side, was ten to twelve inches deep; the bank shelved abruptly to about six feet. Sandy was perched up on the bow at the time so I took the opportunity of speeding up and directed the boat to the shore, hitting the bank at about twelve knots. On impact, the boat shuddered to a stop and Sandy found himself airborne, flying through the air with the greatest of ease, only to splash down in the shallow water.

31

There is no doubt about it, Sandy had performed the greatest harp-over-oboe parabola the world has ever seen; it is just a pity no one witnessed such an astounding act of forced agility but myself.

I waded in and got him back into the boat and told him not to try and emulate the figure head of Nelson's flagship anymore. Needless to say he decided that it was safer to remain in board; however, I constructed a small platform so that he could sit with the forepaws resting on the bow surveying much to the amusement of those fishing in the other boats.

Although personally I have never fallen overboard, it was inevitable that at some time Sandy would experience an unscheduled ducking; most times he made the shore but on two occasions it was touch and go. One was when I had hooked two grilse on the troll at the same time; with the skirl of the reels he got so excited he lost his balance and overboard he fell into deep water, in more than one sense of the word, so I dropped the rod and with the landing net I landed a wet and frightened wee dog. It took some time to sort things out, but eventually we reached the landing stage with dog and the fish; not two, as could be imagined, but four, the other two were caught as we were leaving Polloch Bay. On unloading the catch I noted that my next-door neighbour had his binoculars firmly poised in the direction of the landing stage. At the time he was unable to go fishing, but there was no doubt that he and his family had enjoyed the fruits of the labours of another.

I began to feel that the strain of running the fishing station was too much at my age, so when my nephew purchased an estate with fishing on the Deveron and offered me the position of fisheries manager, I sold the cottage and made a move to the North East. There I was ensconced in a cottage, with duties to welcome the fishing tenants and to see that they were comfortable in the cottages allocated to them; and later, to give them details of recent catches; the state of the pools; the level of the river and where the fish were lying; the flies to use; and finally to wish them tight lines.

As in the case of dogs reaching such an age Sandy began having fits; if out walking he would keel over on his side, become quite rigid, and howl for a few minutes, then he would recover and continue walking as if nothing had happened. Indoors it was a different matter, if he was on a chair or bed he shot off and belted round the room, crashing into anything that came in his way; just as suddenly as the fit had come on it was over, he would then seek a lap or a place by the fire and proceed to go to sleep.

I had only been in residence for a short while before I noticed the "wee man" had no inclination to go walking; he would saunter out into the garden and did the jobs he wanted to do, then return to the house and lie down by the fire. My nephew who has always had dogs, generally two whippets and a lurcher or other breed, noticed that Sandy was getting very aged and to save me having to make the sad journey to the vet, he kindly offered to do so. He took Sandy in his arms and I gave him a little piece of steak and that was the last I saw of him. He was buried in a secluded part of the garden and I planted some daffodil bulbs which will come up each spring to remind me of a wee dog who was my faithful companion for over fifteen years.

LONG ODDS
A story of trolling for summer salmon
and a tale of two fish at the one time!
Reprinted by kind permission of The Gazette Group

'ONE day when spring was slipping into high summer with a blue sky above and billowy white clouds being hustled along before a spirited breeze; the boat was pushed away from the jetty and the outboard motor started.

We, that is to say, myself and Sandy, a Jack Russell-Border Terrier cross, had six miles to cover before reaching the fishing area chosen for that day. Running before the wind and skimming down the rolling waves built up by now a really stiff breeze, it did not take long to reach our goal. Dapping, however, was out of the question so we had to resort to trolling.

The larger of the two motors was raised and the 2 h.p. model lowered into the water. It is an ideal size of engine to propel the 15' 6" boat along at just the right speed to make the lures work at their best. Fifty yards of line, to which gold and silver lures attached to 9ft of 20lb B.S. nylon, were let out from each reel, then lead weights were placed on the line to make sure that the hooks went home, should a fish take the lure.

With everything set and an eleven o'clock beer poured out, there was nothing else to do but sit back and enjoy the rocking of the boat by the waves, which by now had increased before the rising wind to make almost perfect conditions for trolling. In a matter of minutes they proved so to be; the rod bent and the reel screamed, as, far behind a flash of silver revealed a fresh run fish.

Sandy was by now scampering from stem to stern, yelping his head off and generally getting in the way. The boat was now heading for a rocky point and had to be manoeuvered round it using one oar; then the strong wind caught it on the beam and eventually the keel grounded on a gravel shore without damage. By this time the fish was under control, and gripping Sandy by his collar he was unceremoniously thrown overboard, to swim the few feet to the shore, this action allowing me to net the fish without any trouble. It was a grilse of about 5lbs and covered with sea lice, which proved that it was straight up from the sea.

With the trolls reset it was decided to go into the next bay, which at this time of the year has the reputation of holding fish. The waves were being squeezed through the narrow entrance by the force of the wind and they were nearly three feet high. There is a well known salmon lie at this point, so with conditions as they were it came as no surprise to see the rod point bend towards the stern and to hear the welcome sound of the running reel. The engine was cut, but the waves were carrying the boat forward at speed towards the shore and an overhanging blasted oak tree under which we came to rest.

The slack line of the other rod was blown up into the branches and the bag of the net got caught up also, however the fish was fairly well played out and lay on its side allowing the net to be freed and used to get the fish inboard. Sandy would not allow himself to be caught, so it was some time before order was restored. It was near lunch time so we headed for a sheltered spot on the shore and hauled the boat up, taking care to tie the painter round a large rock.

Queen Anne supplied a much needed dram to go along with smoked salmon sandwiches followed by biscuits and cheese, of which Sandy demanded his fair share. By the time we had finished lunch it was impossible to get the boat off the shore, so it was decided to wait and see if the wind would subside. After about an hour we managed to get afloat and made for the open water so as to be able to put out the trolls again. This done we went back into the bay and did one circuit which was uneventful. As it was getting late it was decided to do a final one then head for home.

Just as we were leaving the bay at the narrow part aforementioned, both the rod points swung back and the reels screamed in unison. To hook one fish in such stormy conditions is bad enough, but to have two on at once is a challenge to be met with a cool head. Before the first fish was netted, not without considerable difficulty, the boat was ashore bow first which was most fortunate. It was some time later before number two could be brought under control, because it had run out so much line. In time, however, it came along side and was safely gaffed; it had to be used because the first fish was in the net with Sandy sitting on top of both of them.

Confusion reigned, the fish by now were slithering around the bottom of the boat, the lines got tangled together, and got even more so with Sandy chasing the fish and then getting himself caught up in them. There was only one thing to do; get him untangled and again throw him overboard, so into the water he went! The fish were knocked on the head and eventually everything was all ship-shape and Bristol fashion. With the gear stowed away and Sandy back aboard, we made for home and a happy landfall.

The four grilse weighed 25½lbs and they were quickly deposited in the deep freeze unit.

It was ten days later, under similar weather conditions, that a trip was taken to a point eleven miles up the loch. Again the wind was too blustery for fly fishing. The trolling area consists of two large bays and a long rocky face under which the salmon lie very close inshore, but despite careful trolling over the several lies, nothing happened. During lunch time the wind dropped, as it does in these parts, and it was possible to use the dapped fly, as a result a sea trout of 2½lbs came to the net.

As luck would have it the wind failed completely so the trolls were set for a quick sweep round the upper bay. With little to do but call for the comfort of Queen Anne, a dram was enjoyed which made up a little for the disappointment of the lack of wind. Now comfortably settled and musing over fishing days gone by, both good and bad, the screaming of the reel suddenly broke the reverie and called for immediate action. After a furious fight the fish came towards the boat, and it was then spotted that the lines were crossed and, moreover badly tangled; nevertheless a successful netting of the fish was accomplished, much to the delight of Sandy who immediately attacked the slashing tail.

It was fully ten minutes before the lines were disentangled to enable the second rod to be lifted and the line reeled in. In doing so however, there seemed to be a drag on it; thinking the lure had got caught up in the weeds a good heave was given to the rod. At that very moment a fish jumped out of the water some 70 yards away. In due course the fish came to the gaff and was landed successfully. The catch for the day was three grilse, 24½lbs and one sea trout, 2½lbs.

In reviewing the two days fishing, the end product was most pleasing, but what was even more so was the fact that on two occasions two fish came on at the same time and that they were all successfully landed. The chances of such a happening in a life time are long odds indeed and may well never occur again, to myself or any other angler. A case perchance for the Guiness Book of Records?'

DO WOMEN MAKE GOOD ANGLERS?

A good question, and I have a good answer to it, it is Yes, with a capital Y. My mother, as the old adage expounds, use to say "If you can't beat them then join them" and after she had joined my father, they used to plan a fishing holiday each year, staying at the many fishing hotels around the North of Scotland.

They also paid visits to Loch Leven and enjoyed at that time, when conditions were favourable, the catching of twenty-five to thirty trout, both during the day and especially in the evening sessions.

It being more comfortable, my mother would be seated in the stern and with a 9' 6" split cane rod and a short line she cast out from the stern and drew the flies in front of the boat, where the natural flies accumulated in the calmer water.

She kept the boatman busy landing the trout, whilst the bow rod caught his quota, but at the end of the day, the better basket almost always fell to the rod in the stern. It is a pity that such an outstanding loch had to suffer the effects of pollution and fertilisers which are conveyed into the loch in the wet weather by the many small feeder burns, which run through the treated fields.

My daughter had to join the club, otherwise she would have been left on shore. We were staying at Ardsheallach Guest House and we decided to go fishing one evening. It was getting dark and she said "I think I have caught something," so I took the rod and confirmed that there was a fish on the end of the line. She then took over and round and round and round the boat the fish went, picking up the green ribbon weed. In the darkness I shone my torch to show where the fish was; eventually it came to the net.

There were six other anglers staying in the house and on making enquires before my daughter returned as to how they had fared that day, I learned that they had only two finnock between them, so you can imagine the gasps of astonishment as Gillian walked in with a 5½ lb. sea trout held up for everyone to see.

The Queen Mother is an ardent fisherwoman as everyone knows, and it is said by those who have seen her, that she casts a no mean fly. A woman of my acquaintance is an exceptionally good performer of the art and devotes herself entirely to river fishing, showing no fear whatsoever when it comes to wading into the quick running streams of turbulent water.

She and her husband travel around in a Range Rover with two large dogs and how they manage to find room to lie down is a mystery, because the back is crammed full of fishing tackle and I have never seen so many rods, possibly they are slightly over stocked, but it is better to be prepared for all emergencies.

I have seen her standing thigh-high in swift running water, hook a fish, gradually back out onto the bank, gaff or tail the fish in the quickest time I have ever witnessed. Her husband is a jolly good fisher, but if I were a betting man my money would go on her every time.

When I was at Acharacle I had to take out two women of middle age, who had hardly any fishing experience and certainly not of dapping. I fitted them out with rods and flies, then off we started in favourable conditions to a nearby drift.

Never have I heard two human beings natter away as these two, they resembled a cage full of monkeys, until one rose a small sea trout, then concentration took over and hardly a word was spoken except my giving them instructions and encouragement.

By way of conversation I said if I happened to be a psycho-analyst and had a singularly difficult case to treat, I would recommend my patient to take a fishing holiday and try for salmon and sea trout. They gasped and said "But we are both psycho-analysts." Really quite a coincidence!

Another woman angler visited me on several occasions; apart from being very experienced she had a shocking habit of falling asleep at the drop of a hat. It so happened that we were well up the loch suffering a strong wind so we decided to change beats to a more sheltered one. No sooner were we under way than her head fell on her chest and snores could be heard above the wash of the boat.

When we reached our chosen drift I shouted to her to wake up; eventually she came to and stood up to get onto the cross seat, but lost her balance and sat down on top of two dapping rods, two fly rods and trolling rods. After examining the damage, her rod being a metal one it was straightened, whilst my hollow fibre glass one was crushed, but with some wrapped tape, was made serviceable. Fishing proceeded, but the atmosphere was not as jolly as it had been previously, until we both saw the funny side of the happening, which was capped with a couple of drams.

BOATS AND BOATMANSHIP
By kind permission of The Gazette Group

'There are thousands of boats in use and, owing to the popularity of just messing about in and around them, and the great desire to go sailing or fishing on sea or loch, the number will be ever on the increase, as the recent Boat Shows have proved.

My own experience has, in the greater part, been with loch fishing boats, and it is this type of craft about which I want to write and attempt to give a few hints and tips in handling them, and in general some ideas of boatmanship.

The old adage which states that there are no bad whiskies, but there are some better than others, unfortunately does not apply to loch fishing boats. They fall into a great number of categories, ranging from well built, well maintained and well behaved boats, to badly designed, ill cared for and thoroughly ill-behaved tubs.

It is difficult to understand how an owner, be he a private person or an hotel proprietor, can imagine that a boat will look after itself, but judging from what I have observed and experienced, this fallacy seems to exist in the minds of many of them.

I kept a boat on Loch Lomond for several years. She was 12ft 6in long with a 5ft beam, little free board with a 1½h.p. Stuart Turner two-stroke inboard engine. She was a splendid sea-worthy craft and was well behaved on the drift. If there was a slight cross wind, by altering the weight of the boat, she would crab-walk down the drift in a most exemplary manner. If there happened to be a really heavy cross wave, she could be kept on the drift by gently pulling on an oar, the one in the wake of the drifting boat.

In winter I used to haul her up into a sheltered corner of the boatyard and take the engine out. The keel rested on pieces of good hardwood, with struts of sound timer pressed into the ground and slid under the rub rail on either side to keep her steady, then with a final check to see that the cover was well secured, I left her.

I found it advisable, however, to run down now and again to see that all was well. In dry, frosty weather the cord of the cover would slack away and if a wind got up before a snow or rain storm, it could be wholly or partly lifted off.

A few hours work on the engine in the garage was all that was necessary to make sure it would be serviceable for the next season. The work on the hull was a different matter.

Whether a boat is painted or varnished, a considerable amount of scraping and rubbing down will have to be undertaken. Blisters and scrapes break the finished surface and moisture can creep a long way under the coating. It is not until this is disturbed that the full extent of the non-adhesion comes to light. Only when the edges are smoothed off and the bare patches are thoroughly dry, is it safe to apply coats of paint and varnish. If the weather has been damp, but at times dry enough to undertake painting, the planking may require caulking between the seams. Should the plugging up of a crack or seam be overdone, it can result in further opening in one or both directions, as the packing is apt to swell under the water line, or in wet weather conditions.

If the boat was watertight the previous season, there is no doubt that it will be again; however, it is better to put her in the water close to the shore until the planks have swollen, before installing the engine. To bring her down to the normal water line without the weight of the engine, a few heavy stones can be used. The extra work involved is likely to be much less than drying out the engine, if, foolishly, it had been put in before launching.

A final check over fittings and the tightening of screws, etc., is also necessary before she is ready to serve for another season.

Some hotel and association boats are better cared for than others and if they do suffer damage, it is often due to the ignorance and carelessness of the person who has hired one for fishing or other pursuits. Having baled the boat and loaded in the gear, she should be shoved off until afloat provided there is a jetty of sorts. When embarking from a staging or pier boarding should be made by placing the foot in the middle of the centre thwart and then move to bow or stern to allow others to come aboard.

If there is no jetty and gumboots are worn, get the boat afloat and enter by stepping over the gunwale as near the centre of the boat as possible. Then move to the stern and with the handle of the oar, not the blade end, be prepared to shove off. Your partner should press down on the bow to counteract the weight in the stern, then shove off and come in over the bow as near the centre point as possible.

The fishing, other gear and the lunch basket, should be stored away in the bow and covered with a ground sheet or some similar cover, to prevent rain or spray wetting it. Surplus gear, such as petrol tins and tools etc., should be placed under the thwarts, well out of the way.

Few fishers venture forth nowadays without an outboard motor of some make or another, the majority of which are so designed to fit on to the transom of the average boat. Boats of recent construction are in the main designed to take the engine, but on more than one occasion I have found the holding bolts on the engine bracket could not be opened wide enough to slip over the transom; in the first instance by a mere ¼ inch. A small amount of wood surgery with a strong single bladed knife soon rectified the fault and the engine was fitted without difficulty. In the second instance, nearly ¾ inch had to be removed.

A lesson had been learned and, the following day, I purchased a small wood chisel, which I carry in my tool bag to this day and which I have used on more than one subsequent occasion. Surely the owner should have seen to it that the boat, which was for hire, would take a standard outboard motor bracket.

When placed in position, the thumb screws should be tightened thoroughly, then with stout rope or chain attached to the engine, it should be secured to the stern ring, round a thwart or any other part of the boat giving a sound fastening. Many outboard motors lie at the bottom of the sea, lochs and lakes, just because this simple precaution had not been observed.

The petrol tank should be filled, if not already full — a tin of spare fuel and the tool bag should be aboard. In the bag, apart from the tools for the engine, there should be at least two spare plugs, two shear keys or springs, a length of starting rope and a small selection of copper or galvanised nails in a tin, a length of 2in wide bandage and a small container of quick drying varnish.

A leaking boat can be a pest at all times, but a quick repair can often be undertaken with the latter mentioned kit.

If no outboard motor is available a check should be made before leaving the landing stage to make sure that the oars are serviceable and that they are complete with rowlocks.

It is as well to inspect the oars to see they are not over worn at the point where the oars rest in the rowlocks and that there are no obvious cracks. They should be fitted with a leather collar so as to prevent them slipping through the rowlocks into the water, which can so easily happen when your back is turned.

If no band or collar exists, the next best thing is to tie the oar to a strake or rib inside the boat with a piece of cord. This method, however, restricts the use of the oar when pushing the boat off the shore. Alternatively, the string can be tied round the waist of the rowlock which is just below the 'U' fork — the oar can then be lifted along the rowlock and used to help shove the boat into deep water.

However, it is not so important nowadays to have a pair of matched and balanced oars working in well fitting rowlocks, because, apart from the occasional row home, should the outboard motor cease to function, they are really only used to steady the boat on the drift. I would, however, hate to try and row the boat more than a few yards with some of the ill-matched pieces of wood purporting to be oars, which are placed in the boat for use by the angler.

There are several types of rowlocks — the conventional kind, the single and the two-pin rowlocks, and I have seen a rowlock screwed to the oar on a universal joint, the pin of which slips into the rowlock hole in the gunwale.

If the latter type was more frequently fitted, it would be a great boon to the hirer of the boat.

The rowlock shank differs in diameter and the holes differ in size, so if you get a boat with large size holes and rowlocks with thin shanks, you are not in for a very happy time. The rowlock will probably rock and this is one reason amongst others for "catching a crab", because the oar jumps out of the rowlock, which will have tilted.

Ill-fitting rowlocks of this nature quickly wear the lower hole, normally drilled in a piece of hard wood fitted between the ribs of the boat, thus increasing the rock which, in turn, makes the boat unrowable, except in the calmest of conditions.

POACHING

Poaching is a crime and is dealt with by the law. Unfortunately the penalties often do not fit the seriousness of shooting game, deer, or netting and gaffing game fish without permission. The miscreant is often let off lightly and so the evil practice continues.

The age of youth is not taken by the law as an excuse if you are caught in the act, or found with a salmon in your possession as a result of your activities, so it is better to be on the safe side and stick to normal activities. Nowadays, because of greatly depleted stock, a stricter outlook is being kept by gamekeepers, ghillies, and riparian owners themselves to protect their property.

At a very early age my two friends and myself were fishing a small river with worm. The water was low and very clear, and as a result we were not having much sport until we came up to a long narrow pool, in the middle of which were three salmon. We had a consultation and decided to pop a worm in front of the fish, but it was as good as hopeless, and there was little chance of catching one of them; so we decided to throw in a stone to see what would happen.

The fish darted for cover and in a second none were to be seen, then I spotted one of them lying vertically against a clay bank on the other side of the river. I have never seen camouflage used to such good purpose; the fish conformed to the curvature of the bank and its skin seemed to reflect the greyish pink of the clay and thereby it became almost invisible.

On our side one fish was not so lucky; it was visible and very vulnerable, lying just below us. It was too much of a temptation; a worm was allowed to swim down towards the fish. Just at the right moment it was jerked up and the fish was caught, much to our delight. One out of three was not too bad, so with that thought in mind we packed up and made for home. It was a very mild case of youthful poaching.

In the late 1970s when trade was booming and manufacturers were busy, the angling section of the employees were having it the

43

"McMillan Way". It was nothing for a party from the firm's angling club to fly up to the outer isles late on a Friday afternoon; bivouac at the lochside; fish most of the night; rest during the morning; resort to fishing again during the night, then take the early morning plane back to Glasgow. A short fall in pay packets at the end of the week, seemed nothing against a weekend's poaching. This just shows what some people will do in their desire to catch fish.

"One for the pot" has been the axiom amongst almost everybody who was privileged to live near a river, and in most instances a blind eye was turned by the gamekeeper upon the practice. That was in the old days, but now with the price of the river salmon being what it is, the habit of taking a fish now and then has got out of hand. Instead of the poached fish being eaten by the family, they are taken to the hotel where a back door deal is concluded.

The Ayrshire coastline is relatively free of islands; those which are there are in the main large and do not provide hiding places for poaching trawlers. In contrast, from the Mull of Kintyre to Scourie there are hundreds of islands which provide cover for the poachers of which there are many in the area; despite the presence of fishery protection vessels. Heavy catches are made with the deadly small mesh nylon nets; there is no doubt that this persistent netting of salmon and sea trout accounts for the disastrous reduction in the lochs already mentioned.

Many of the Scottish rivers are heavily poached but none so much as the river Tweed where organised gangs, helped by spies and lookouts, have wrought havoc with the fishing the length of the river.

When fishing out from Lochmaddy Hotel we went to a brackish loch, but apart from seeing a sea trout, about 4 lb. in weight, grubbing in the seaweed and turning over stones with its snout for grubs, the boat was clean. Charlie, our ghillie, suggested tramping over the moor to a small lochan about a quarter of a mile distant. We walked up by the side of the outflow burn, where we spotted a trap fashioned out of wire frame covered with a small mesh wire netting. At the downstream end, the netting formed a funnel so when a fish entered, it could not escape. The up burn end was closed with netting. Charlie pulled it out and carried it some distance away across the moor, stamped on it until it was flat and hid it as best he could in the heather.

After all this palaver it was decided to return to the hotel without anything to show for our efforts for the first time during our stay.

A great number of coarse fishermen came up from the Midlands to fish the border rivers complete with their stools, umbrellas and a plethora of tackle, and the inevitable cans of worms and maggots. The course fishing is really very good in the river Annan and it was there I first spotted the umbrellas, just one or two, not like the forests of them as often seen on TV.

Most of the local anglers do not object to the visitors from the South, but they are a little dubious as to what has not been put in the keep-nets and could find its way into the boot of the car along with the clobber of tackle being loaded in preparation for the journey south. Only a custom's man could verify of what the catch, if any, consisted, but no such control is in existence at the present time, but what if the Scottish National Party has its way?! Perish the thought.

A small spate river was in order, so I decided to go over and ask permission to fish for the day. I was rather early so when I crossed the river over the old bridge I stopped and had a look; there, with its head hidden by the bridge arch, was a splendid grilse. In case the river was running too big for fly fishing I had taken the precaution to have a few worms with me.

It was blowing quite hard up stream which suited my purpose, as the baited hook would be blown up stream hopefully ahead of the grilse. I let out line then the worm disappeared but as it floated down, a small finnock took it. I pulled it to the other side, unhooked it and let if go. Having baited the hook again I repeated the operation and this time the line tightened. I gave it a jerk and all hell was let loose, my fish dashed downstream, disturbing two others which jumped and darted about the pool which now looked like a mill race.

My problem was getting down from the bridge to the bank in order to play the fish, which was made difficult by a holly bush growing out of the side of the bridge. The wind blew my line into the middle of it, and I therefore let off a length of line from the spinning reel and carefully dropped my rod onto the bank. When I got down I retreated a short distance and pulled on the line which fortunately came away. I was able to play the fish to a standstill; at last, much to my satisfaction, it lay on the bank.

I thought it wise to hide it close to the wall up at the road, whilst I sorted out the tangle my line had got into. At that moment a telephone engineer's van drew up and I heard the door slam, the driver appeared with a kettle in his hand; as he passed me to fill it with water he said "That's a braw fish you have caught, the early bird catches the worm so the speak." He went back to the van and disappeared, much to my relief.

I proceeded to collect my permit, only to be told that the general was in his bath, however I had not to wait long before he appeared. I paid my dues and thanked him, then left for the river. By the time I had to leave, it was with three sea trout to make up a satisfactory catch for the day.

Strictly speaking I had poached that grilse because I had not permission to fish at the time, however, my mind was relatively untroubled as I drove back home.

THE WRONG TURNING

I had heard from a friend that the fishing out from Garvault Hotel, at the time owned by a Mr MacKenzie, was very good; with a selection of hill lochs, the Baddanloch and a stretch of the Helmsdale just below the sluice gates; these control the water flow for the main river. We set off for the North in happy anticipation and eventually made ourselves known to mine host, who introduced our ghillie to us; he turned out to be a splendid fellow.

The weather conditions were variable so a council of war was held before breakfast to decide where we would fish during the day. The hill lochs provided good sport and so did the Baddanloch until, for days on end we were blown off. Thus the river and a small deep peat stained burn remained the only places to fish.

All good things must come to an end so on our last day we decided we would fish the river and the wee burn which had offered up some of the plumpest, most beautifully coloured "trooties" I have ever seen, and very edible as a breakfast dish. It was these speckled beauties that Gordon went after, leaving me to fish the river.

The ghillie mentioned that my friend was very disappointed at not being able to take a salmon home with him, so it was up to me to make a supreme effort to catch one for him. During the process I caught a 2½ lb. salmon straight up from the sea. I then traversed the sluice to fish from the other bank where I caught a 1½ lb. trout. Time passed quickly, as it always does when fishing, and I was becoming concerned at not having caught anything worthwhile. The ghillie and I had a conference; a quick look through my tackle provided the answer and very soon a 7½ lb. salmon was landed and hidden in the heather, near the path to the sluices. No sooner accomplished than my friend appeared looking very pleased with himself as he emptied seven trout from his basket; he then asked how we had got on and he accepted our, "not so good" reply. It was then time to go back to the hotel so we packed up and started to approach the sluice, my friend leading the way. Imagine his surprise when he tripped over the salmon hidden in the heather.

A dram or two in the bar and the ghillie departed on his way and my friend ordered an early breakfast. He came to my room in the morning and said goodbye; I wished him a safe journey while I stayed on to fish a further day. On my return to the hotel I was met by a glowering MacKenzie. I sensed that there was trouble in the air, so I quickly asked him to have a drink, which he accepted and then related the following happening.

It appeared that my friend in his haste to get to Edinburgh had taken the wrong turning and found himself in Bettyhill which is equidistant in the wrong direction from the hotel as is Helmsdale.

With foot pressed down on the accelerator in order to make up lost time he sped southwards. At a bad bend on the road he met MacKenzie who had gone down to Helmsdale to get a trailer load of coal. With a screeching of brakes and swaying of cars, my friend disappeared down the road leaving MacKenzie more or less in the ditch with a partially tipped trailer and coal spread all over the place. With the help of a passing motorist the car and trailer gained the road and the spilt coal reloaded then both proceeded on their ways.

It took more than a dram to resolve the situation; the others in the bar sensed the atmosphere between the two of us, not to mention an amount of eavesdropping by them which led to MacKenzie producing his violin from under the bar; he was a grand fiddler and proceeded to prove his expertise well into the night.

It was a late start I made for home the following morning, thanks be to St. Christopher — the Saint of Travellers — in the right direction.

DO THEY GO TOGETHER?

It is a matter of choice, some anglers like to take a bottle of whisky with them in the boat, whilst others prefer non-alcoholic beverages. The weather conditions have an important bearing on the matter. One can get so chilled when harling on the Tay in January all feeling in the limbs ceases to exist, but a dram at such times helps to resuscitate the functions of the body. In addition this can be helped when the reel screams and a fish is on the end of the line.

Drinking for drinking's sake can be a dangerous pastime and there is no doubt that many boating accidents can be attributed to excessive consumption. I witnessed a fishing party of four on Loch Leven, when one member stood up he fell overboard. With difficulty he was pulled on board by the others. From their behaviour all were obviously the worse of drink and it was only 9.20 a.m.

The weather conditions can change so rapidly; one moment a gentle breeze with a sun warming the atmosphere can change to a cold wind causing a drop in temperature. Those who have not taken proper waterproof and warm clothing with them can be chilled to the bone in a very short space of time, so a dram on occasions such as this is most welcome and could prevent unpleasant repercussions of one sort or another.

On a club outing on Loch Vennachar some time ago, two members who should have known better drifted before the wind. As they passed they were singing at the top of their voices, arms round each other's shoulders. A bottle of whisky was held in one hand from which they alternately took swigs. They passed on their way rounding a point and disappeared — they were not present at the weigh-in.

With the stricter drinking-when-driving regulations now in force, at least the driver of the car has the sense not to drink to excess before taking the wheel. As for the passengers it is entirely up to them to do as they please.

The disposal of empty bottles is always a problem — they should not be left lying around, as there is always a risk that small boys will use them for target practice with air guns or catapults, and on no account should be broken on purpose. A solution was found by a boffin-type friend.

When the dam at Loch Monar was completed, a large metal mooring buoy was left at the lower end in a bay near one of the two dams. The bottles were loaded into the boat and we made for the buoy which the boffin grabbed with one hand; with the other he got hold of bottle after bottle by the neck and smashed them against the buoy and the bits fell to the bottom of the loch. He had nearly completed his task and picked up the second last bottle. There was a loud explosion and the boffin suddenly realised that he had smashed his bottle of lemonade which he had left in the bow of the boat overnight.

A TIT FOR TAT

It was a business-cum-not too serious a fishing trip that Bobby Muir and I arranged. Off we went and made some calls on our way to Aberdeen. We were warned that the town was very busy and it would be wise to book our rooms by telephone. Having got through to the receptionist I asked for two single rooms in the names of Mann and Muir, but could I get the girl to understand? I could not. Getting a bit hot under the collar, I said "Book the rooms in the name of Manure" — Sure enough, when we arrived and went to the desk, the booking had been made in that name.

Bobby drove the car in an almost stop and start fashion. One moment his foot was on the accelerator and the next on the brake, to a point that it got on my nerves, so after lunch I took the wheel. On the Huntly-Aberdeen Road there is a well-known underbridge with the railway passing on top. It was before the traffic lights were installed, so I proceeded at speed down the hill. On a previous occasion, I had noticed a farm road ahead running parallel to the railway line, and with foot flat down on the accelerator went straight on up this road. Bobby stiffened, attempting to put both feet through the floor boards and when we stopped he was speechless. I then backed out and went through the bridge and on our way. I turned and asked Bobbie "Would you like me to stop and buy you a drink?" We did, and it was only after he had two stiff ones that he said "Please never do such a thing again to me!" I agreed, feeling the score had been settled.

THE ART OF TROLLING
Reprinted by kind permission of The Gazette Group — July 1974

'Trolling is just not a matter of letting out one, two or sometimes three lines and proceeding up the loch.

To start at the beginning, proper equipment is necessary, a suitable boat and a well-serviced and reliable outboard motor. Good waterproof clothing and a well-padded boat seat adds to the comfort of the angler. A net, at least 24in. in diameter with a deep bag or a gaff head with a wide gap, both fitted to shafts of not less than 5ft. in length are essential and finally a priest of decent size.

In detail, the rods should be not less than 10ft. 6in. in length and stiff. The reels not less than 3in. in diameter, with lines of a minimum length of 200 yards. A nylon trace about 6ft. long of between 16/20lb. breaking strain with a ball-bearing swivel fitted between the line and the trace.

A good selection of spoons, minnows and wobbling lures will make up the necessary equipment.

The lines should be marked at 40, 50 and 60 yards by painting on a little nail varnish, then wrapping silk thread of different colours round the line and with some more nail varnish between the thumb and forefinger, rub the thread and then leave to dry. The best type of line is rotproof of man-made fibres and between 25/30lb. breaking strain. A feature is that there is very little stretch in such lines in comparison with mono-filament nylon lines of any breaking strain.

Two or three lead weights or smooth stones covered with either cloth or leather are the last but not the least important items.

If there is a choice of boat it should be about 14ft. to 16ft. long with a good beam. Make sure that there are either rowlocks or stops on the gunwale for the rods. A cork with a 2½in. nail driven through it from end to end and then hammered into the gunwale makes a satisfactory rod stop. It is sometimes difficult to secure the rod butts.

If, however, there is a thwart, a loop of string placed round it will hold the butt by slipping it through the loop.

To start trolling, let out the lines a few yards only, then lift the top of each rod and make certain that the lures are spinning or wobbling in the correct manner. It is strange how the treble hooks can get caught up on the line and sometimes the swivel gets kinked at the split ring, which if trolled in this way would lessen the chances or even give no chance at all of catching a fish.

Having let out the lines to the required length, place the lead or stone weights on them, but be careful not to leave any slack. The check on the line will help to drive the hooks home.

The outboard motor must be able to tick over steadily and the cooling water must flow through the engine. In some makes this is not always possible, so a metal or fibre disc 2½in. less in diameter than the propellor should be clamped or wired on to the blades. This will allow the motor to rev at a greater speed and the water will circulate. At the same time the boat will be driven at a suitable trolling speed.

Before setting out on your fishing trip and if you can find the whereabouts of a set of bathymetrical survey maps of the Lochs of Scotland (there are such maps to be found in the Mitchell Library in Glasgow), it would pay dividends to make a rough sketch of the loch which you propose to fish and shade in the areas of between 12ft. and 25ft. in depth. Also mark any isolated banks or spits around which the fish are prone to lie. There is a bank on Loch Shiel which lies 100 to 150 yards offshore and which is known to few, but was discovered by referring to the maps in question.

In low water the bank can be clearly seen and the bottom can be touched with an 8ft. 6in. long oar. Many good fish have been taken off this bank by those in the know. There are few if any lochs in Scotland that don't have such banks and they are difficult to find, their location being closely guarded by the local fishermen. Sometimes if a fish is caught the ghillie will remark: "It is strange that a fish should be caught so far out, she must have been a traveller."

It has been known for some anglers to troll all the time, despite good fly fishing conditions, whereas others only troll when there is insufficient wind for fly or so much wind no other method of fishing could be employed; but if you must troll, the best conditions are a good steady breeze, changing light or a rip-roaring rain storm. On one occasion, returning to the jetty against sheets of rain and a high wind, I let out the trolls and in the space of two hours, three fish were hooked. One was lost at the net, two were landed and the fourth threw the hook 100 yards from the boat.

There are two ways of setting up the rods in the boat. One is the conventional way, with the rods almost level with the surface of the water, which permits trolling in 10ft. to 12ft. of water and deeper with normal type spoon or minnows. If semi-floatable type baits are used, it is possible to troll in much shallower areas, sometimes to great advantage, as salmon often scull around in 5ft. to 6ft. of water.

The other method is the "Hemingway". The rods are placed in special brackets which can be angled, as a result the rods are placed about 45 degrees to the surface of the water. The advantage of such a setting will allow trolling in shallow water with heavier type baits, such as spoons of the "Toby" type, often taken by salmon and big sea-trout in preference to the semi-floatable type which don't flash so attractively emulating a small fish in some sort of trouble.

I have already mentioned that sometimes three rods are used, a method favoured by some anglers on Loch Lomond. The third rod is known generally as a "Poker", but it should not be used unless there are two or more people in the boat, ready to wind in the lines in the event of a fish being hooked.

In playing the fish a good strain should be maintained, but should it want to run, it is best to let it do so, but keep a check on the line so as to maintain control. If the fish is hooked in shallow water every effort should be made to entice it out into the middle of the loch, where there will be no underwater obstacles to foul the line. Many fish are lost through being impatient to see it lying in the boat. It is best to play the fish until it is lying on its side and gradually bring it over the net; never try to put the net under the fish, such a movement could scare it and, still very much alive, it could make a sudden dash which would take the angler by surprise and possibly the line could snap or the hooks pull out. Take your time, but don't overdo it, because the hook could, with all the twisting and turning lose its hold and there is no more sickly feeling than a slack line.

Do not imagine, because you know that the area in which you are trolling has a nice clean bottom and free from weeds, that the hooks will not get foulded up with something. It is easy for a twig, a piece of grass or weed, even the paper from a cigarette end or sweet, to meet up with the line and slide down it to foul the lure. It is therefore imperative that the lines should be brought in from time to time and the lures examined to see that they are clean.

When trolling with a wobbler type of lure, the movement, as it is drawn through the water, is transmitted up the line, which causes the rod tip to vibrate rhythmically, thus indicating that no weed or other substance is impeding the normal movement of the wobbler, therefore keep an eye on the tip of the rod to make sure that the lure is making it vibrate all the time.

This, however, does not apply when fishing with a spinning

minnow, but as the boat is being driven at an even speed, the bend on the rod should be constant, however should the bend increase gradually or even with a sudden jerk, the indications are that weed has been picked up or a fish so small that it hasn't the power to run the wheel, so an inspection of the lure is called for.

It is a bit of a thought to have to wind in 50 or 60 yards of line, so it is better and quicker to hand-line it in and lay it neatly on the deck of the boat. If a ball-bearing swivel is used you should not experience any trouble with the line kinking; if, however, you do detect the slightest sign put the line back in the water and use the reel. In doing so guide the line on to the drum, so it spreads evenly across and not pile up on one side or another, which could result in a "bird's nest" of no mean proportion and the loss of trolling time.

The line picks up a lot of water when trolling and more so if a fish has taken off 100 yards or so. Therefore at the end of the day or period of fishing, wind the line on to or round something such as a chair or mantelshelf and let it dry. If you think the line is twisted, tie one end to a post or tree and walk away letting the line off the reel and lay it on the ground, then walk back and unhitch the line, return to pick up the reel and pull the line through the grass which will remove any kinks or twists. Then rewind the line on to the reel and dry as already mentioned.

If there are two or more persons in the boat and the other line is safely wound in, immediately man the oars to be ready to follow the fish should it make a run. By doing so control is kept over it and it will not be necessary to recover so much line.

When in a boat by oneself there are two methods of handling the situation when a fish is hooked. One is to grab the rod and strike hard to make sure the hooks are over the barb. Stop the motor. Put the rod down in such a position that it won't be pulled overboard should the fish decide to make a run for it. Reel in the other line as quickly as possible and lay the rod down with as much of it inboard as possible, so your line won't foul the tip when playing the fish.

If the fish has been hooked near the shore with a wind blowing strongly towards it and you are by yourself, forget about the fish, get on to the oars and pull for deep water. It is better to lose a salmon than to damage the boat and the outboard motor. Generally speaking, however, if the fish has taken the bait properly it will not be able to throw the hook and as it feels no strain the desire to fight against it does not exist, so when the rod is picked up again be prepared for a fight.

It is strange how many fish when hooked run towards the boat and this is where a large diameter reel aids a speedy recovery of line. If, on the other hand, the fish goes off in the opposite direction, the reel will house plenty of line, which can be torn off at such a rate it is not possible to see the handle going round. A run of between 150 to 175 yards is not uncommon by a fish straight up from the sea.

The other method is to pick up the rod, cut the motor or put it into neutral and proceed to play the fish in the hope that the other line won't be fouled, or at least not become so badly entangled as to cause the fish to be lost.

When at last the salmon or other fish is safely inboard, sit down and take stock of your position. If you are too near a rocky shore get on to the oars and pull well out, because sometimes it takes quite a while to dispatch the fish and take out the hook during which time the boat can drift a long way in windy conditions. It is best to keep the fish in the net so as to get a good grip of it and with the priest or other suitable article, give it several good raps over the head to make sure that it is dead. It is sometimes very difficult to remove the hook and if the fish is not quite dead, a shake of its head could drive a hook into your finger or cause a deep ragged scar.

In any loch there are certain areas which hold fish and there the anglers will be found. So, if troll you must, look out for these fly fishing down a drift; never go too close and above all don't disturb the water in front of the other boat.

Always give a wide berth to another boat trolling. Some anglers troll with monofiliment lines and often do not realise how much line is out and it has been known for the boat following to pick it up with either the propellor or even the lure.

The boat in the lead always has the choice of fishable water, but one unsavoury type of an angler thought otherwise and crept up behind the writer, overran his lures, revved up his engine, then veered off having severed his lines. A heated argument ensued and he accused the writer of crossing in front of his boat, a poor excuse for such behaviour.

The person in question has always trolled at about 1½ miles per hour, whereas the normal trolling speed is about 3½ miles per hour. In fact, he had increased his speed on purpose, so his was a deliberate act, an act of an utter cad. It was a sad breach of angling etiquette.

To end on a more cheerful note, more salmon appeared around the coast and both in rivers and lochs during 1973 than for many years past, and they came readily to the trolled lure and to both wet and dapped flies. This could be the result of recently introduced controls governing fishing in the sea, reduced pollution in rivers, better husbandry by riparian owners and members of angling clubs and associations.'

PIKE

Loch Cluanie has always lured me to its peaty water, so over a holiday weekend three of us loaded up the car and sped north. Some of the gamest trout and some of the largest pike inhabit the loch. Both species can be fished for at the same time; wet or the dapped fly can be used for trout and a football bladder attached to a wire trace with a large hook, baited with a piece of meat for the pike.

We set two of the pike baits in a narrow inlet, much like a canal, then set off to catch trout on a drift along the north shore. We had decided to fish until lunch-time and return to see if by chance a pike had been tempted to taste the meat. To our satisfaction we spotted the bladder half submerged and moving about in the narrow waters; now how to land the cannibal was the question.

We threw stones to try and get the fish to come near the shore, but to no avail. I suggested to Bunny to get his rod and put on a large fly. He selected a Greenwells Glory size 8 which he cast up wind of the bladder, while I threw stones to make the fish move towards the fly line, which it did; the line tightened and the fun began.

The pull on the line and the resistance of the bladder through the water soon tired the pike; as a breed they are not known for their fighting qualities. After about a quarter of an hour the fish was netted and laid in the heather on the bank. It proved to be a fair size so we decided to go up to the inn to weigh it. As we walked along the bank to the car we spotted that the other bladder was up on the bank, but how did it get there was the question. We theorised for some time, but could not come up with a satisfactory answer to the query. We arrived at the inn and asked for a weighing machine; the ones we had did not register above 10 lb. However, Frank Robson, at that time owner of the place, produced a scale used for weighing the carcases of deer. We hung the fish on the hook, saw the indicator drop to register the weight of the pike as 22½ lb., not the biggest the loch has produced, but a fair specimen none the less.

Sandy

The Catch

Pike

First of Season

All this activity aroused the interest of those in the bar, so they came out to have a look. One inquisitor came over to view it and observed "The other pike isn't so big as this one." He added that he had been bank fishing and found the bladder of the other one stuck in some weeds, and being curious as to what was on the end of the line, pulled the fish high up the bank, knowing that in time we would discover it.

So, after some well-earned drinks, we returned to the loch and after our lunch we continued to fish during the afternoon. Determined to make the most of our short stay we had our evening meal and went out to fish the evening rise with a reasonable result and then so to bed.

SKIPPY AND BEANIE

When Sandy died I lost no time in trying to find a replacement, the more so because I live alone and I must have a companion to keep me company.

I phoned all the Cat and Dog Homes without success but when speaking to a friend she mentioned the name of one I had not tried. I was in luck. The voice at the other end of the phone said "Yes, we have a Jack Russell and if you are here by midday the dog is yours." I was down at the Home in double quick time and there he was, a splendid youngster. Having concluded the transaction we were on our way home.

The dog had a stupid name which I did not like, so I waited for a day or so to see what type of a character he was. Rather than run he seemed to skip along at the rate of knots so he answered to the name Skippy from then on.

He enjoyed his runs up at the golf course where I lunch daily when in Glasgow. On one day he disgraced himself by falling into the River Kelvin which circles the course on the north side. My difficulty was how to get him out, because he had dropped down a five foot vertical bank onto a ledge he could just stand on. I made a lasso out of a long lead, I then managed to get it over his head so with the aid of my walking stick up he came.

At home he behaved in a very normal way and settled down in no time at all. I enjoy my early morning cup of tea, after which I went to have my bath, the tea tray being left on the bedside table. Having dressed I went to cook my breakfast only to find the milk jug was empty. How he managed to lap the milk out of a narrow necked jug had me beaten.

Another time I had set the table for dinner and there was butter, and a chocolate mousse for a sweet, the telephone bell sounded so I dashed to answer it. Before I had got back the mousse container was empty and there were little tooth marks on the remaining half of the butter. After these episodes, all edibles were kept beyond his reach.

I had him for about a month when, one day exercising him in one of the many Glasgow parks, he ran up to and went through a high link mesh fence in answer to the bleat of a goat. I called him and he came to within a yard of the place he had entered when out of the blue three Borzois came bounding up and set upon him tearing him to bits. I was on one side of the fence helpless. As there was nothing I could do I returned to the car and went home. I sat down in my chair and wept.

I phoned my daughter and she retrieved the body from the owner of the dogs who said it was my dog's fault, he should not have gone through the fence. It was pointed out the dog had died because he had not mended the hole in the fence. Skippy was duly buried in my daughter's garden.

So my search for another dog began again and it was a long one; however, I eventually became the owner of a one ear up and one ear down Jack Russell; he had already been named Beanie and by Jove he lived up to his name. He was everywhere, doing a steeplechase course round the room, over chairs and the settee and under the table. Once he got used to the flat he calmed down a bit and began to behave himself. He also fell into the Kelvin but only needed a little help from me to get onto dry land.

At that time I was going north to look after the fisheries on the Mayen Estate for my nephew. I lived in a small cottage with a garden and a patch of lawn upon which Beanie did a bit of self-exercising; round and round he went always on the same track so it was not long before it became nearly two inches deep. There were other dogs around the place so he was not lonely.

One day when up at the golf course I walked him along the canal bank but he got the scent of a bitch and refused to come back to my call. The last I saw of him was a dot in the distance and still going until he disappeared. I got back to the car and had a snack lunch. I told two of my friends to look out for him whilst I drove along the tow-path (strictly forbidden), at the end of which was the main road. I decided to visit my daughter and tell her the sad story. On the way there is a double bend and it was round the second that I saw Beanie in the middle of the road. I sounded the horn and he came running towards the open door of the car. He must have travelled nearly two and a half miles from the time I last saw him. Imagine my joy at finding him, as he might have been run over by a car on that busy road.

My neighbour has a cat and there is a cat flap in his door, with an open catway in the main door. I had returned from walking Beanie who was behaving in the way of all dogs having got the scent of a bitch on heat. I took Beanie off the lead at my front door having closed the other, but before I could say Jack Robinson, he was through the catway and vanished.

I went in search of him but without success and returned to the flat half an hour later to find Beanie lying on the door mat, his side covered in blood. He whimpered as I opened the door and proceeded to limp towards the fireplace. I did what I could for him and decided to telephone the vet; the phone was out of order and my car was being serviced. I gave him a closer look over and decided there was nothing badly broken.

In the morning, we went off to the vet. Beanie was X-rayed and given the normal antibiotics' injections. The plates showed a tiny fracture which mended quite quickly, but even after ten months he occasionally limps along on three legs. He is a very lucky dog to be alive today.

It was sad that Skippie did not live long enough to experience the joys of being out in a boat watching fish rising and being brought into the boat. On the other hand, Beanie has fished Lock Brora and the Spey. He sat contentedly snuggled up on the lap of the ghillie whilst I cast, and, like the disciples, toiled and caught nothing.

"A COLOSSAL COINCIDENCE"
Reprinted by kind permission of Scot Rail

November, 1962

A colossal coincidence involving two "C.C.'s" — that's the only way I can describe the experience of my late father, Charles C. Mann and my brother — also named Charles C. Mann. Each of them caught trout . . . each trout weighing more than 10 lbs. . . . and as illustrated each foul-hook by a fin.

There will be no better way of describing how this came about than to quote the article which appeared in the *Fishing Gazette,* of February, 1936. It was written by my father, and is reprinted by kind permission of the *Fishing Gazette.*

A PRIZE

Many friends who have heard of the unusual capture of my heaviest brown trout during the period of my thirty years of angling, have mentioned that I ought to send the story up to some of the sporting papers. I had no time to devote to writing this during the summer and, I daresay, it might be more enjoyed if read whilst sitting over a cosy fire in the winter time.

One nice morning my wife and I left Tongue Hotel along with our ghillie, called John. The weather had changed from a long spell of gusty south-west and west winds to one of south-east. When we were all ready in the boat we made for the lower and of Loch Craggie, and having heard the previous evening from an angler that he had hooked, and lost, a nice salmon that day, fishing a small sea trout size of teal and green, I thought the same one ought also to be my tail fly for the day. Up till about 12 o'clock we had managed to pick up some nice brown trout and the light and conditions were

61

improving. Coming to a part of the loch where a point runs well out, and having fished the windward side, John suggested reversing the boat and that we might fish the other. I requested him to give my wife the best water, that being the edge of the bank — one might easily expect a salmon to rise here; for my own part, I never thought of a fish where my flies were as it was only two to two-and-a-half feet in depth. However, I lengthened my line so as to get my cast away from the boat as far as possible: my rod was a twelve foot Greenhart, and an old and valued friend of thirty-two years. The cast was 2X with three flies. Presently I thought I saw a movement of a big lad and struck — "I've got him and a good fish" I remarked. Away he went taking off a good 70 yards — he stopped when he got near to the shore and I recovered some line. Off again along the shore and this sort of thing went on for several minutes. I began to wonder why it was I could not get him turned to head the wind. I asked John to steady the boat and I would tighten on the fish, always keeping in mind my 2X cast. I also was beginning to be anxious over the fact that he was going towards the outlet of the loch all the time and that Mr. Salmon was no doubt keeping that in his mind. After putting on a good strain I got a sight of him, it was only a fine big broad tail that was waving to me, and forty-five yards out — marks on my line showed me this. He was foul hooked for certain and a fish of about twelve pounds we all agreed. Out from that shore he would not come and the wind was freshening. What was to be done? John remarked that we could not kill him where we were and I also stated that I would be happier to be away from the outlet stream — this passes into Loch Slam, which is always full of salmon. Looking to the wind-ward there was a nice sheltered bay on the other side, a good quarter of a mile off. Nothing for it but to try to get him to come with us. With the fish in shallow water, naturally the line was straight out from the boat. So off we started, John was going very slowly to see if he would come. Up to this I had had fairly good fun, but now it was a different story — worry was in my mind as I was determined to get that fish. Patience and skill were called for from us all. A good twenty minutes had gone up to this point. Slowly we went and then I could see the line becoming more upright; the fish was played out and sinking and was following along the bottom. He must be among large boulders as I felt him bumping over them quite distinctly — I remarked to John, "What if he gets jammed in between stones?" All this time I never gave way an inch of line, but the strain began to feel too great — my 2X gut! The rod was bent to its limit, my left arm ached, being cramped and tired — our friend was pretty well drowned by now. At last I had to give, or something would have to go. I gave a matter of five yards of line, which meant in all 50 (150 feet). Sounds deepish!

The line had become almost perpendicular — this was the deepest part of the loch we had. On we went like the snail and soon I looked round and said, "Not long now John." The boat was run aground and the fish was away out behind which meant he was also getting into shallower water. The bumps were also getting more severe. I found that I could not use the reel, so there was nothing for it but to drag the fish along a yard or so and lower the point, then reel in the slack. The drag was heavy and great care had to be taken, still every moment meant he was coming nearer. The 20 yard mark was seen but soon he almost refused to move, so care was necessary so that I would get him over the hurdle — evidently a boulder. This proved to be the worst one. Another rest had to be taken so that my arm could be straightened out. In a little while up came the cast loop and we all gave a sigh of relief and joy. My wife looked at her watch and said, "Forty-five minutes" and John began to smile. I heard him quietly remark "Here he comes" then we all saw the big fellow. A fine broad side and his tail still working slightly. Now for the gaff. Well placed by John and a lift saw our friend into the boat. The teal and green was firmly into the body end of the ventral fin. So as to let the people in the Hotel see it for themselves I got my scissors and cut the gut a couple of inches from the fly. Meantime, while my wife and John were looking and admiring, I proceeded to collect my cast and to hook the middle fly into a ring and get my rod put down. To my astonishment I found the precious cast in two places — broken below the "bob" fly. How, when and why remains a mystery, as John had not touched the cast when gaffing. I was busy tying it up when I felt a hand on my knee and John remarked, "Mr. M. you have got a greater prize than a salmon, he is a beautiful big brown trout." I then looked over his shoulder for I was in the bow seat, and sure enough he was right. A perfect specimen, lovely shape and colour and best of all a very neat and shapely head for a cock fish. I put the age down at something between eight and nine years. There he lay being discussed and admired — John said he had never seen in all his long experience (over 40 years) such a fish taken from any of the Tongue waters. "A record fish too, Sir." This made me feel more bucked than ever. My wife read the time on her watch as fifty minutes and not too soon as far as I was concerned. Patience rewarded! We got ashore, it now being one o'clock. All drank to the wonderful "kill." Our ghillie could not have been more skilful or patient in the work that he had to perform and "I take my hat off to him." It all required careful work and knowledge. The cast had lasted out. This was purchased from Mr. John MacKay at Thurso a week or so before and was supplied to them, I understand, by Messrs. Redpath of Kelso —

surely a record also, one might say. Mr. MacKenzie of the Tongue Hotel was, of course, greatly pleased when he set eyes of the "Craggie Monster" and after a chat we both decided to send him off to Mr. John MacPherson, Inverness, to have him "set up." Very soon a model will be seen in the hall of the Hotel. The actual weight turned out to be 11 pounds.

Truly, a lucky day, and one never to be forgotten.

C. C. M.

Brown trout, 11 lbs., caught by C. C. Mann, senior, on Loch Craggie, August 17, 1935.

Brown trout, 10 lbs. 8 ozs., caught by C. C. Mann, junior, on Loch Quoich, June 2, 1959.

TWENTY YEARS AGO
Reprinted by kind permission of The Gazette Group

On 2nd June, 1959, while fishing a well-known West Inverness-shire Loch with his brother and Mr W. M. Cook, Mr Chas. C. Mann of West George Street, Glasgow, had the remarkable experience of landing a 10½lb cannibal trout on the fly.

Mr Mann rose a ¾lb brown trout, which showed itself, and was in the act of playing it when suddenly the weight increased and his line was run out to the backing. It was presumed another fish had taken one of the other flies on the cast, and it was 30-minutes before the evidence came to the surface in the shape of an enormous tail lashing the water. When the fish was eventually netted and taken into the boat it was discovered that it had been foul hooked by the second fly ('Woodcock and Hare's Lug') at the base of the right pectoral fin.

The cast was made of 6lb breaking strain 'Luron 2' and the three flies tied on as a "Dundee" cast (i.e. no droppers). The rod was a 9½ foot two-piece Walker Bampton, and a 3½" reel by the same maker.

The first fish got off in a struggle so it will never be known if the cannibal had endeavoured to catch the smaller one and got caught up in the process, or whether the whole thing was an accident!

E

METAL FATIGUE AND MIRACLES

After running a fishing station for twelve and a half years, and approaching eighty-two years of age, it was decided that enough was enough; the decision was made even more positive when an offer was received, and accepted, to manage one and a half miles of the river Deveron near Huntly, Aberdeenshire. Without more ado I was on my way, not on a bike, but in an overloaded car and trailer.

I was free to go because the cottage from which I had been running the fishing station had been sold in rather unusual circumstances. One hour after having put up the "FOR SALE" notice at the gate, I spotted a lady walking down the driveway. I went to meet her, and after introductions had been made she asked if she could see over the place. She was obviously impressed by what she saw because as we walked towards the gate she enquired about the purchase price. She made no demur at the figure mentioned and said, that subject to negotiations,she would like to buy the cottage; a speedy transaction by any standards.

On arrival at the place of my new employment I was allocated a cottage which needed some renovation, so whilst staying at the "Big Hoose", the alterations were planned to begin in the spring. Before leaving for Glasgow for the winter, I surveyed the river and estimated what had to be done to make it more attractive to those coming up to fish the following season.

When I came north again in April of the following year, I had firstly to get estimates for the renovations; which included installing central heating, redecoration throughout, fitted carpets and rewiring. Once they were accepted I had to supervise the work because there was little time for completion before the end of May when, thereafter, VAT was to be charged on all home improvements.

As the work progressed satisfactorily, attention could be given to the river bank. With assistance, steps reinforced with timber were constructed at two very slippery tracks down to the river-side. At six strategic points, bench seats were erected. There is nothing worse than trying to change a fly, or take out a wind knot when standing up on a windy day; not to mention not being able to sit down in some comfort on a seat.

The river-side paths had been sadly neglected, so with pick and spade, cuts were made into sloping sides in order to widen and level the paths for easy walking. Duck boards were fabricated and laid across ditches. The making of easier and safer walking is an insurance against accidents and damage to rods. The three huts, one at each end of the beat and one positioned in the middle, were in good shape and little had to be done to them. It was most gratifying when the fishing tenants arrived to hear them say how much they appreciated the improved facilities.

Once safely settled in the renovated cottage, it was possible to get the rods set up; make up casts; inspect spinning gear; and then it was down to the river bank. My Jack Russell Terrier, "Beanie" by name, led the way and could not get there quick enough. He found the banks of great interest, following the scent of otters, mink and all the other inhabitants. At times he disappeared into the hinterland to chase rabbits, returning every now and again to find out if I was still around and had not fallen in.

It was on one of his return journeys, soaking wet, he shook himself with his usual vigour, making his identification disc tinkle against the metal parts of his collar. Suddenly there was no sound; I looked down and there on the ground lay the two halves of the split ring with his "medal" lying on top. A matter of metal fatigue and most fortunate that it happened at my feet.

Before I sold the other cottage, in Acharacle, my nephew and I were out on Loch Shiel trolling for salmon when suddenly the reel screamed and he picked up the rod. From then, the fight was on; the fish shot off at the rate of knots and then, when it was being retrieved, quite near the boat it made a sudden plunge to the bottom of the loch. There was a PING, and the line shot back over my nephew's shoulder. On examination of the tackle, all that was left was the swivel, the split ring at the spoon had fractured. After a moment of contemplation I heard him murmur "Metal Fatigue"; a very modest remark in the circumstances.

The following recorded incident has nothing whatsoever to do with fishing, river management or metal fatigue, but as in the million to one chance of "Beanie's" disc falling off at my feet, it is another very long odds bet.

One Saturday afternoon, after a very good lunch of the five-course variety — four double gins and a plate of soup — we were standing on the tee, to the right of which is quite a famous doocot lying in a direct line of a well sliced ball. It had suffered many a direct hit and one ball had lodged between the guttering and the stonework. I had already remarked upon this oddity. The others apparently being reluctant to drive off, I addressed the ball and took an ungainly swipe at it; it shot off the toe of the club towards the doocot and lodged within twelve inches of the other ball.

I am perfectly certain that if the details of this feat were to be fed into a computer in order to ascertain the odds against the repetition of such a happening, on pressing the button for the answer, the bewildered machine would have blown its top.

FREAK WAVES

Freak waves occur in all the oceans of the world; they also happen in certain river estuaries, take the Severn Bore for a good example. Inland waterways are no exception, some of the worst freak waves have been experienced on Lochs Maree, Lomond and Shiel.

They are not created by a blustery wind, but by a steady pressure which builds up the water into big rolling waves, seldom breaking into white water at their peaks. The worst can be experienced where the loch narrows, or between islands; they proceed, and seem to increase the further they travel up the loch.

The worst I have ever encountered was up at the Black Rocks on Loch Shiel. The wind was not extreme at this point, but it can only be presumed that further up the loch it was blowing harder and had built up the wave which we experienced. I noticed a misty blue line which partially crossed the loch, more pronounced on our side of the loch, than the other; as it approached I said to my partner, "Get down on the deck." I slowed the motor, maintaining steerage way and then it hit the boat; up went the bow, over came the water (most of it went down my partner's neck, as he complained later); then the boat came down in the trough with a thud, proceeding into less severe conditions.

The wind lessened, and we proceeded to have drift after drift with fish showing all over the bay; my partner was having great sport. I had to keep the boat on the banks where the fish were most active, but I also managed my fair share of the catch. When it was time to make for the landing stage, it was then we blessed the rolling waves; we just roared down the loch, going from one wave peak to another, spray spreading out on both sides. When we came alongside of the landing stage we agreed that we had experienced an exciting day with a splendid catch of salmon and sea trout. It was a day to remember if ever there was one.

On another occasion when a stong gusty wind was blowing making it impossible to fish we took refuge behind an island. There was another smaller one nearby on which a blackthroated diver had built its nest, so we poled the boat round to have a look. We proceeded without making a sound, as we thought, but just as we came in sight of where the nest was, the bird close to the ground came sliding down through the grass and weeds into the water leaving not a ripple as she sank down out of sight. We did not investigate further, it was sufficient for us to know that the birds had returned to breed for another year.

Two anglers fishing Loch Awe had an alarming experience and it could have been caused by a freak wave.

On some of the larger lochs, and those which have been flooded, and where they are surrounded by farm land, dividing walls between farms and fields were built out into the loch during times when the water was low. Some had wire fences set on top of the wall and iron posts were used instead of stobs, which would soon rot.

Where the bank shelved quickly, the wall went a short way into the loch, but if the shore was flat it could go out some considerable distance, and this also applied to the wall and the fence. It was while their boat was drifting over an extended wall that the freak wave hit it and lifted the boat high on the crest. When it descended there was a bump and a crunch of timber, the post had split a plank letting the water rush into the boat. Fortunately another boat was following behind and those in it heard the shouts for help, downed rods and rowed quickly to rescue the doomed fishermen, who got off with nothing more than a severe drenching. If the other boat had not been to hand it might have been quite another story.

A freak wave could have had a hand in what happened to my plastic mug, one of the first of its kind and given to me at the Engineering Exhibition which was held in the Kelvin Hall in the early 1950s.

It was the last day of the season; my brother and I set off for the Black Rocks and at lunch-time we landed, heading for our favourite luncheon spot. When we left we packed everything into the lunch case; it is made of plastic over a 10 inch × 10 inch frame about 14 inches high. As there was no wind we set off home; half-way down the loch I felt thirsty and looked for my mug but it could not be found, however the top of a thermos flask satisfied my needs.

At the beginning of the following season Jimmy Wood and I made for the Black Rocks; on the way I said "Jimmy we will be landing for lunch at a special place." He asked, "Why?" so I replied "Wait and see!" We clambered up through the knee-high heather, and there, before my eyes, was my much treasured plastic mug. It must have been a mighty high loch and a mighty high wave to have washed the mug so far up the bank.

I was lucky to retrieve it, and I may add, that after thirty-six years I still enjoy my dram from the same plastic mug.

CARE OF TACKLE

Some anglers take great care of their fishing tackle, whilst others do not seem to bother about the condition it is in; the latter are the losers in the long run, not only tackle wise, but badly kept tackle can be responsible for the loss of many fish.

It is much better at the end of the season to service all tackle before storing it away for the winter, this applies to the fishers of game fish; the coarse fish angler operates usually during the winter months so these suggestions do not apply to them.

The recent developments in the manufacture of nylon, braided nylon and plastic coated lines means that it is not necessary to dry them because they are almost rot proof. However, every care should be taken to dry them at the end of the season. One method is to wind the line over the back of a chair and when it is all off the reel, tie a short length of string round the skein of line so that it will not tangle when being handled, then hang it up in a convenient place. Silk lines should be dried every time after use.

The whippings on the rod are the places where, with the flexing of the rod when casting, signs will show of the varnish cracking, and also where it has come in contact with the gunwale of the boat when not in use; this damage is done mostly when motoring in rough weather conditions, so the whole rod will have to be varnished.

Do not use a brush to varnish the rod, but put a little of it between the thumb and forefinger of the left hand, grip the tip of the top section, and gently turn it whilst your fingers gradually work down to the ferrule. Repeat this two or three times allowing the section to dry between treatments. The middle and butt sections should be treated in the same way. The cork handle can be cleaned by being rubbed lightly with a fine grain sandpaper which will remove the grime from it, and in the end, your rod will look like new.

The spools of the reels will have to be removed and with a small paint brush, dipped in petrol, carefully clean the inside, removing all traces of old lubricant and small particles of foreign bodies. When dry apply with the brush a very small quantity of light lubricating oil on the spindle and ball bearings, and do not forget the handle; put a little oil on the spindle.

All the spinning lures should be removed from their boxes and laid out on a sheet of newspaper and thoroughly examined for any damage caused to the flights and hooks by coming into contact with rocks when casting, or being caught up in the bottom of the river. Bent or blunted hooks should be straightened and sharpened. It is also important to examine the net for any holes which may have been made when in use; also test the bag for strength as dampness can rot the fabric.

Make sure that your waterproof clothing is dry, then hang it up and spray it with water proofing liquid from a spray can, or brush it on. Leave the clothing to dry and give it another coat, particularly along the seams; at least three coats should be applied to these vulnerable parts. Finally, keep the clothing on the hangers and place in the "cupboard under the stairs" or some other convenient place.

Most anglers have an excess of tackle, a lot of it carried in canvas fishing bags; quantities of grit and dirt accummulates in the pockets which eventually can get into the reels often with disastrous results when playing a fish. Thoroughly clean out the pockets of all extraneous substances. It is better to leave the bag empty, and place all the tackle required for the next season in a box so that you can see exactly what you are loading into the bag before leaving on your first fishing trip.

If an oily floatant has been used on the dapping flies it is best to remove it by holding the fly in tweezers at the spout of a steaming kettle; not only the oil will be removed but the hackles of the fly will be stiffened. When dry, spray the flies with a floatant liquid and then place them in a bug-proof box, the floatant will then be absorbed by the feathers, which is a good feature. The canvas fishing bag should also be sprayed at the same time.

All this work is very much worthwhile, and when spring comes there will be no panic then because you know your tackle is in perfect order.

COMPETITIVE ANGLING

A good number of years ago I was invited to join the Phoenix Angling Club and thereafter I enjoyed many club outings and got to know the members, many of whom are now my friends. An air of companionship existed along with a spirit of competitiveness without any of the needle that can be witnessed sometimes in other sports.

There was one instance when an excess of keenness prompted the secretary to fish in one of the Loch Leven Competitions, but as a very junior member of the club, and having won the club championship, by rights I should have gone to the Loch. It was my sponsor who told me, otherwise I would not have known anything about the matter. I may add such an incident did not occur again.

Petrol was cheap in those days, but at times it was difficult to get it, so whenever possible, we made up a party and drove to wherever the outing was taking place. This led to greater companionship and to talk over the doings of the day; which flies had been used, and where the fish had been caught, completing an enjoyable day's outing.

In time I became a director, and eventually President of the Club. In my year very unfortunately the secretary died so another had to be found. This was not very difficult as the club was well known.

The outings were mostly confined to fishing the following lochs; Leven, Vennachar and Lomond, so it was thought that some new venues should be tried. It was agreed to try Lochs Faskally, Tay, and a new reservoir situated in the hills above Lochgair. The results of the experiment were not very successful and not appreciated very much by the members so the meetings were arranged for the following season at the old venues. I am no longer a member of the club but I understand that meetings now take place at the Lake of Monteith and Loch Fitty; this was largely due to the disappointing catches from Loch Leven when the loch suffered an overdose of fertilizers and pollution. As I write, it is gratifying to know that the fishing has improved and a visit to the loch is now worth the journey.

I once had a splendid catch there on a day of cold north-east winds (a favourable wind for the loch) but it was steady, which allowed the boat to drift off the shallows into the deeper water. There was action both in the morning and afternoon with a dull period midday. The sixteen trout wighed 19½ lb. and my partner was not so far behind. Our boatman (not ghillies on Loch Leven) were contented because he had won the boatman's prize.

My resignation from the club came in a strange way; the first of the incidents occurred at an outing on Loch Vennachar where for some years I had booked a boat for each Saturday. It was a 16 foot boat, very well behaved. I arrived early and put on the outboard motor and loaded my tackle and gear into the boat. When the secretary arrived he came down to the water's edge and said "You are allocated boat No. 6," to which I replied "I am sorry but this boat is not available, I have it booked every Saturday." No matter, I had to take off the motor and shift my gear to the other boat, which was quite unmanageable in all weathers.

At the weigh-in I was standing near the secretary who shouted "Any more fish to be weighed?" I was having trouble taking off the cast from the line so I said, "Here you are — catch" and threw the fish to him. A few days later I was informed that I had behaved in an ungentlemanly manner.

The last straw occurred when I received an anonymous phone call. On lifting the receiver a female voice said — "Mr Mann the secretary said that you are winning too many competitions, and in consequence you are 'non persona grata' in the club. This assertion was no doubt based on the fact that I had just won the cup and all the other club trophies presented that season.

I resigned, followed, by a number of other members who could no longer stand the unpleasant atmosphere which now prevailed in the club. For some, the club was dead.

It was on a private visit to Loch Vennachar with a friend that an amusing incident occurred. It was snowing hard (such conditions seem to excite the trout and good catches can be made during such a storm) but we continued to fish. On nearing a scrub-covered bank, a pheasant shot out of the undergrowth and flew in front of the boat landing with a splash in the water in front of us.

David shouted to the other rod "Quick cover it," whereupon with a relfex action out went the cast and the unfortunate bird was hooked, but after a struggle escaped — so did out thoughts of roast pheasant for Sunday dinner. We came to the conclusion that the bird had been wounded and that was why it had floundered into the water.

QUESTIONABLE FRIENDS

The friends you meet in the normal run of life seem to be just quiet human beings, but on certain occasions they can show quite a different side to their natures, whether it be playing golf or going fishing. We had a Sunday morning foursome and played come rain or shine — it was during one of these games that one member showed up in his true light. He had driven into semi rough and his ball finished up behind a tree; he walked up to it and kicked it with his foot so that he could club it to the green — people do green things at time.

Another friend confessed to my brother that he "could not stand that brother of yours" and on being asked "Why then do you go fishing with him?" he answered "Because he puts me into fish." I had done so on many occasions when fishing with him on Loch Cluanie. With the flooding of the loch, the lapping of the waves washed away the soil between tussocks leaving shallow indents in the shelter of which the flies got trapped and the fish went in after them.

It was a matter of guiding the boat close to the shore and the rod could then be cast blind over the bank landing on the flies in the lagoon — if a fish was in there feeding on the flies it was ninety-nine per cent certain that it would be hooked, it would then dash for the open water and would have to be followed and played there. Having repeated this operation on three different occasions resulting in three fish of 3½-2¼ lb. and 2 lb. being netted, shows what he meant when he said "Because he puts me into fish."

As an organiser of many fishing trips of a day's duration up to a week or two, the other rods are apt to do little to supply the wants of the party; one chap fishing on the Saturday said he would return on the Sunday with food to join another friend of mine for whom I had provided the necessary supplies. When it came to drinks' time, I handed the bow rod his liquid refreshment and just as I was about to lift my glass to my mouth I found a hand outstretched ready to grasp it! He had forgotten to uplift his packed lunch before leaving the house. Apart from this mishap we caught fish and we finished up having had an enjoyable day.

It is generally accepted that the ghillie is the recipient of the gentleman's drams, but in my case it was different. I enjoyed a glass of beer at eleven o'clock and a wee dram with my lunch; but it was a little awkward for me to be drinking in front of my tenant(s) for whom I was ghillieing, so to save embarrassment all round I would offer a drink, which was accepted more often than not.

One day the two rods I had out with me were not shy in accepting the drinks I offered them. Having downed them, we proceeded to fish resulting in a nice basket of sea trout. At the landing stage in the evening it was suggested by one of them that next day they would provide the whisky.

At about 11.45 my tongue was going like a bell clapper and I wondered how long I would have to wait for the promised dram. It wasn't until we landed that I was asked if I would like a drink, to which I replied in the affirmative. Imagine my surprise when, from a waistcoat pocket, the 'pocket pistol' was produced and a few drops of preheated whisky was poured into my glass.

Having eaten my lunch I absented myself along with Sandy, who wanted to have a stick thrown for him. During the operation, and out of sight, I fortified myself well for the rest of the day, which I spent on the oars with a contented feeling in the pit of my stomach.

A fishing competition is held each year on Loch Shiel — anglers coming from far and near to compete. One competitor was over ninety years old and had fished the loch for many years. He put his name down along with two other competitors who would be fishing from the same boat. At the weigh-in he produced the basket which consisted of a great number of parr caught by the three rods which was not permissible, nor were the parr, but it won second prize. The same thing happened the following year and the result was reported to an angling magazine claiming a record for the ninety-two-year-old angler.

The third year however he was not in the running so the rules were changed to read "the total catch of the rods in the boat will count," in the hope that again he would be in the prize list, but even that manoeuvre did not bring about the results expected. If a competitor is not prepared to fish fairly it is better for him not to compete at all and the organisers should have know better than to allow a basket of parr to qualify for a prize.

OUTBOARD MOTORS

I first became acquainted with outboard motors when I joined a fishing party on Loch Shiel in 1947. There were three of us in the boat, and, having finished the drift, the motor was started up. It was the most junior of the Seagull family. In normal weather conditions it could propel a boat with three persons in it in adequate fashion, but faced with a fair sea, and being driven onto a lee shore, was asking too much of it, so the oars were manned to lend a helping hand to the wee Seagull which responded valiantly.

My first outboard was an Anzani which introduced me to the troubles one can expect from the tribe of outboard motors in general, but, to be fair, they were largely of my own making, although they are very temperamental. I failed to take that facet of their behaviour into account. In the end, however, having gained experience, I eventually got of level terms with Seagulls, Johnsons and Evenrudes. Rowing home from eleven miles up the loch against a fair wave is not a pleasant pastime but it sometimes had to be done. In many instances the failure of the engine is due to plug trouble; sometimes they get oiled up simply because the choke has been left partially closed; or the petrol-oil mixture had not been prepared according to intructions.

Mechanical failure does not occur very often, but things can go wrong. On one occasion, coming down the loch, I overtook a man on the oars in an exhausted condition. A tow rope was attached, and we reached the landing stage safely. Later it was discovered that the crank shaft was broken; on examination a fault in the metal was found.

Carelessness and stupidity play a large part in the mishandling of outboard motors; sometimes it is the fault of the owners, and, on occasions, the hirer of the machine. To go out without spare shear pins or springs is asking for trouble, especially when fishing any lochs which have been dammed where there are many underwater obstacles and, if hit by the propellor, a shear is almost inevitable.

When landing for any reason, the outboard motor must be raised, because when the boat is hauled up the motor shaft is dragged into the shallower water; then, when shoving the boat off the shore, the kedge will dig into the ground and damage to the propellor can occur. Worse still, the gearbox can be split and fall apart if care is not taken to avoid underwater obstructions. To my knowledge this happened to two Seagulls; unfortunately both belonged to me.

I hired one of my Seagulls to an angler, who returned before I came off the loch — I found the motor on its bracket in the autoport and when next I wanted to use it, I found that half of the gearbox casing was missing. The hire fee did not cover the cost of the repair by a long chalk, and what I thought about the man who hired the motor, had better not be printed.

A most unusual cause of trouble is cavitation. Some boats have unusual sterns which are not noticed when attaching the motor, however, when underway, and especially at speed, the propellor draws the water away from the stern, and instead of it cooling the motor there is only an air space. This will result in the engine overheating, resulting in the possibility of a seizure and a row home; not to mention a costly repair bill. A lesser damage could occur to the seals in the gearbox; this did happen to one of my engines. However, all this can be avoided by setting the cant of the shaft further away from the stern of the boat in question; this will allow an unobstructed flow of cooling water.

When the fishing season has drawn to a close, that is the time to put the engine onto the bracket, making sure all cooling water has been removed; take out the plug and insert a small amount of oil into the cylinder; this will prevent the formation of rust in the cylinder during lay up time. Replace the plug, but do not tighten. Drain off the gearbox oil and replace it with fresh oil; this done, you will be able to start the new season with the knowledge that your motor will be immediately serviceable and, hopefully, trouble free.

ANGLERS, FISHERMEN AND TACKLE

As in every walk of life there are different classes of people, and this applies equally to the angling fraternity. There are the purists, and the not so pure; those who prefer loch fishing to the river, a fetish to some, a pleasant pastime for others. A further division is necessary, it is the angler from the fisherman; the poacher and the poisoner.

Angling is described in the dictionary as "the art or skill of fishing with hook and line." An angler, therefore, becomes an artist of the sport, whereas a fisherman really goes out with the intention of catching fish, whether it be in fresh water or salt. Finally, whilst their methods can hardly be described as angling, there are evil men who go to the river with nets, gaffs, and worst of all, poisoners of various kinds. If they are caught, the sentences imposed by the courts often do not fit the seriousness of the crime.

The fraternity of anglers does not recognise class or distinction, they can book into hotels of their choice whether it be to fish a loch or a river. Some may have better tackle than others, but they all have the same purpose in mind, to test their skill against the wily salmon or trout whilst surrounded by beautiful and peaceful scenery.

Those who have the finest tackle available generally look after it; such was the case of a miner who was fishing the Ythaan estuary where the water is brackish. The salt in it can damage the tackle unless it is washed in fresh water then dried, and that is exactly what the miner did. Anyone who looks after his tackle in this manner is inevitably an apt angler.

Some others do not seem to care a damn about their tackle, and this indicates that the owner is likely to be a bad and careless fisherman, but he will pay the penalty in due course.

The angler for whom I have the greatest regard is the one who jumps into the car and travels into the hinterland in search of a highland burn. When he finds it, he cuts a hazel stick from a handy bush, ties a length of string to it, and on the other end, a piece of gut, to which a single hook has been attached, and finally a nice juicy worm. He proceeds on his hands and knees up the burn, putting the worm into the stream and guiding it the best he can under the banks. As soon as the line stops, a quick flick of the "rod" will bring a wriggling trout onto the bank. The size of the fish can vary, but many can weigh up to 1 lb. If, however, the one just caught is not keepable it can be unhooked and returned gently to the burn. Had a multi-hook tackle been used, it is almost certain the trout would have to be killed after extracting the hook.

Fishing in such solitude, disturbed only by the sound of running water and the chirping of small birds flitting from bracken to heather clumps in search of insects, is a wonderful experience.

With the skyline broken by the peaks of another range of hills, seen through a blue haze, the sun glinting on some almost unseen loch is a picture in itself. The water rippled by a breeze cools the sweating brows of the fisherman now lying fast asleep in a bed of sweet scented heather, dreaming possibly of having a pink fleshed brown trout for his evening meal; so, if he wants it he better get home before it gets too late.

Some anglers prefer to wade the shores of a loch rather than fish from a boat; in this way he gets exercise, and has as much chance of a basket as the boat rod who will be casting towards the shore, whereas the shore fisherman will be casting out from it, so either way the fishable area can be well covered.

As far as the tackle required is concerned it all depends upon the amount of money one wants to spend; a wealthy beginner buying a complete outfit will have to dig deep into his pocket. The following prices quoted are about average. A 15 foot carbon fibre rod complete with 3½ inch reel and line will cost approximately £10.00 per foot; a net about £25.00; a gaff £17.50; waders, breast £40.00; thigh £30.00; waterproof jacket £65.00; add another £50.00 for flybox, flies, nylon, scissors, etc. A 9 foot 6 inch fly rod, reel and line would require an outlay of around £107.00. A spinning rod and line would amount to much the same price. Fishing bag £30.00. Total cost £735.00, or there abouts.

A complete dapping outfit would cost between £55.00 and £65.00 depending on the quality of the tackle.

Dapping can be practised with a 15 foot 6 inch and over, carbon fibre rod, but do not use the casting line, because the weight of it will pull the floss back down the rings of the rod, so a reel line and floss will be required at a cost of about £17.50.

To use a 16 foot or longer, cane rod, will be most tiring, and likely to put one off dapping for a lifetime.

If one has the time to shop around a reduction could be made especially if one can pick up second-hand material in a tackle dealer's shop or at an auction sale.

The aforementioned tackle would be about the minimum a beginner would require, but as he progresses as a fisherman, and chats with other anglers, the conversation will eventually lead the way to the tackle shop, and once inside anything can happen. I know from my own experience, when I decided to "hang up my rods", I had eight rods, nine reels, a countless number of flies and spinning baits and three suits of waterproof clothing, which proves that it is a slippery slope one descends when entering a persuasive tackle dealer's shop.

DANGER AHEAD

In most of the lochs in Scotland, and particularly in the Outer and Northern Isles, there are dangerous rocks and shallow spits coming out from the shore. Should they be encountered, severe damage could be done to the hull of the boat and the outboard motor, so in the knowledge that they do exist in the loch being fished at the time, great care should be taken, especially when proceeding at speed.

Those who visit lochs regularly get to know the snags, but it is not so easy for the casual visitor; in the latter case if a local with the knowledge of where the snags are in the loch is available he is generally willing to advise and should be consulted; it could pay dividends.

Heavy rain which will cause flooding, and a consequent rise in the level of the water in the loch, can eliminate the risk of hitting a known snag, but a prolonged drought could expose some of which anglers were previously unaware.

In the lochs, which have been dammed to provide water for the Hydro Board Generating Stations, are where the most dangerous snags lie. I have fished Lochs Cluanie, Morar, Monar at a certain level one year, only to find, on returning the next year, that heavy rain or prolonged drought has produced higher or lower levels than normal. Thus I was as wise as any visitor to the loch for the first time and any references to the survey maps of these lochs was just a waste of time.

It was at Loch Cluanie that my friend Bunny Cook sat on an exposed rock twenty yards from the near shore and showing well above the level of the water. Some steady rain could raise the level and the rock would disappear to several inches below the surface. A boatman proceeding at speed with the sun low in the west, would not see such an obstacle, and if it was hit it could be disastrous. One would not care to speculate on the result — the same could happen when a steady breeze could conceal the rock. The top end of the loch is the worst place for jagged rocks and also soggy mounds of heather and tough grass. The former spelled the death knell of countless shear drive springs of the Seagull outboard motor I was using at the time — I lost three in the morning so moved to another part of the loch known to be free of such hazards.

During the late 1970s very severe frosty weather was experienced resulting in the level of Loch Cluanie being at an all time low. When the water was drained off from time to time by the Hydro Board the ice began to sag, but clung to the sides of the loch which in the end looked like an ice-covered elongated bowl; a very strange sight indeed, and a great danger to the deer and sheep which graze the banks. One false step and down they would slither to be trapped at the bottom of the icy chasm.

LOCH SHIEL PAST AND PRESENT

Over the past thirty-two years I have fished Loch Shiel spasmodically, usually in the autumn in order to get the late run of sea trout. Later I purchased a caravan which allowed me to make more frequent visits to the loch. With the aid of the bathymetric map, which was the result of a survey carried out by the Admiralty, I began to find the banks and isolated lies where the fish are to be found.

It was when I built the cottage at Acharacle and started the Creel Fishing Facilities Co. in 1970, that I really began to know the topography of Loch Shiel, not only to my advantage, but also to that of my fishing tenants and other anglers. To drift along the banks was the logical thing to do, but there were other places where fish were inevitably to be found, and many a time I warned tenants to be on the alert in case a fish rose to the fly.

I was often asked how I knew that a salmon, more so than a sea trout, was at that particular spot. I told them that if the depth was right, and also the conditions, there was every possibility that a fish was in the area and might take the fly.

There were about five such lies that I knew of, and time after time when drifting over them a fish would show itself, sometimes to be caught; at other times it would come up to inspect the fly only to sink back in the water. On more than one occasion, when doing the drift, the same fish would repeatedly inspect the fly; it seemed to be a kind of routine just to come to the surface to say good morning, and so often, goodbye! I think this proves that some salmon are wiser than others.

Over the seasons it was astonishing how the fish preferred to choose one fly rather than another. One year it was inadvisable to go out without a natural or an artificial daddy-long-legs, where as the next season they were not so popular. Another season it was the turn of a brown and gold bodied fore and aft fly to use in preference to all others. Then the taste would change to some other pattern, but in the end the general favourite was the black pennel.

The best results were obtained when there was a settled period of weather, with the level of the water in the loch at the correct height — not too high, and not too low. Any heavy, prolonged rainfall could result in a rapid rise which would upset the fish for a day or so, all because of the peat stain in the water, which is always slow to clear. I have know the water to be coffee-coloured to the extent that the blade of the oar was not visible eighteen inches below the surface. This meant that the fish would move to where the water was not coloured and it was sometimes difficult to find in such a large loch exactly where they had gone after a spate, not only to baffle the fish but also the angler.

Not so many years ago drifts such as in Weedy Bay could be gone over with the almost certainty of rising fish and with a good chance of catching at least some; it can now be fished with a definite certainty of coming away generally empty-handed.

Another feature is the continuous thundery conditions which have prevailed, and can persist for weeks at a time; there is nothing more likely to have an adverse effect on migratory fish; they simply go to the deep water and remain there until the atmosphere lightens.

In years gone by, thunderstorms were different, sometimes they lasted for a few hours at a time rumbling around the hills and just as suddenly as they appeared they passed over leaving the air clean and fresh. The result of the passing made the fish come on the take; many good baskets have been recorded in such conditions.

The forestry commission planting programme around the loch necessitated the draining of the surrounding shores but, despite criticism, it had to be done; deep ditches were cut into the peat bogs and that really caused the trouble. After heavy rain the coloured water would flow out into the loch where a dirty scum would form; this would move slowly down the loch on the stream. When that happened it was "I to the hills, my boy, to catch the brownies!"

Up until the end of 1976 the fishing was really very good; to quote from my records "In 1973 in 45 days 102 sea trout weighing 136 lb., 7 grilse 40 lb., and 20 salmon 161 lb." were caught. "In 1974, 82 sea trout weighing 122 lb., and 15 salmon 76 lb." "In 1976, 48 sea trout 59 lb., and 4 salmon 21 lb." At the foot of the last report was added "Thereafter the catches declined to such an extent further records ceased to be kept." To illustrate the decline, a note read "In 1983, in 6 days, five rods caught 3 finnock, and 2 sea trout 5 lb. in weight."

Such was the damage that was being wrought by the draining of the surrounding ground, allowing peat stained water to flow into the loch and polluting its one time clear waters in which the sea trout and salmon previously existed.

A friend of long standing built a cottage next to mine, I think it was in 1974. He had a boat and enjoyed his fishing, but as it deteriorated he became more and more disenchanted; he eventually sold the cottage in 1985.

I know that Lochs Maree, Stack, Eilt and Shiel are no longer the lochs that they were, but, on the other hand, Loch Lomond is very much coming into its own and the reason for this may be the purification of the river Clyde, which just goes to prove that all types of fish require clean water in which to live.

A MIXED BAG

I will complete this saga by relating incidents when living on my cabin cruiser at the Trout Inn at Godstow in the late 1930s and late 1940s.

They were happy days, doing a little fishing, entertaining friends from London and listening to the local gossip over a pint or two; mostly during the weekend. I often bought a leg of ham in a butcher's shop in Thame and boiled it in a beer named "Bung of Misery", because a pint or two over the odds had a disastrous effect on the consumer the following morning, but it gave the ham a delectable flavour enjoyed by my guests.

Opposite the inn there was an island with what I believed to be the ruins of the abbey. A wooden pedestrian bridge spanned the river. During the very hot spell the timbers got dried out and when a customer was crossing he dropped his cigarette end which lodged between two planks with the result a fire started. I smelt smoke and looked out of a porthole and saw what was happening; I got a bucket of water, dashed over the bridge and put the fire out before it got a proper hold — pints all round!

During the war my boat had been looked after at Salters' Yard some distance down river. When the hostilities finished, and having returned from India, where I had been seconded to the Indian Army, I found the food rationing very severe after having fed reasonably well in the mess at the Lahore Depot and on the voyage home. I decided to supplement my meagre rations, so out came my fishing rod. There were one or two Thames trout, pike, chub, perch in the river and shoals of smaller fish — I fished for perch because, having skinned them with considerable difficulty, they were very good to eat after being fried in bacon fat, which was obtained at the inn from an obliging bartender.

One day I caught two perch and was about to return to the boat, when I saw a shadow appear from under an overhanging bank. I dropped a worm just in front of it and waited — at last the trout moved forward and took the bait. I got the fish onto the bank and knocked it on the head and began to think of how I could pass in front of the inn, where people were sitting outside having "elevenses" of one sort or another. I decided to hold it to my chest under my pullover and make for the boat. As it happened, just as I was passing, it came to life and flapped in no mean way, much to my embarrassment, until I got it safely on board. It weighed 2½ lb. and made delightful eating.

Another fish which I managed to catch was a 9 lb. barbel; I took it back to the inn, to be met by a keen angler, who immediately said "Oh this catch must be reported to the Oxford paper," to which I replied "for heaven's sake, No! I am on unofficial leave and I have no rod licence." It was readily accepted by the kindly bartender.

I believe when the fish is cooked it is like eating a cushion liberally sprinkled with pins; however, it did help to supplement the rations for a large family.

There are paintings of game fish, also photographs, but nothing can compare with seeing a Thames trout in its natural habitat. I spotted one when strolling along the bank of a feeder stream; it must have weighed 4 lb. at least. It lay near the bottom, fanning it fins and tail to keep its position against the stream, whilst situated over a bed of pale green ribbon weed which presented an activated backdrop, occasionally exposing a clean gravel bottom through the crystal clear water. I stood for quite a while spellbound and then the fish slipped back slowly, to disappear under the overhanging willows leaving me to ponder over the wonders of nature.

With hostilities over, I felt the desire to return to Scotland to represent a firm which manufactured a rust removal and proofing agent, amongst other products. There was no difficulty in interesting firms, many of which had stored parts used in their normal peace-time production, in favour of materials used for the war effort. The former had become covered with rust whilst in store which had to be removed before they could be used. As business developed I found that I could slip away for a day's fishing every now and again without loss of turnover.

In due course of time I was approached by my nephew who said he would like to buy my business; I agreed and we arrived at a satisfactory arrangement. I remained for two years as consultant to the firm, after which I decided to retire. When I say retire, it really meant that I would do so only to build a cottage near to a loch and start up a fishing station. To retire and have no interest is fatal, an active mind helps to keep one young, so I devoted my time to getting set up for my new and exciting venture.

It was during the next twelve and a half years that many of the incidents related in this book took place, which I hope will be enjoyed by the readers of this book, as much as I enjoyed witnessing them.